THE
BOOK CLUB
MURDER

THE BOOK CLUB MURDER

The Frank May Chronicles

Lawrence Friedman

A QP MYSTERY

QP Books
New Orleans, Louisiana

THE BOOK CLUB MURDER
The Frank May Chronicles

A QP Mystery, published in 2012 by QP Books.

QUID PRO, LLC
5860 Citrus Blvd., Suite D-101
New Orleans, Louisiana 70123
www.qpbooks.com

ISBN 978-1-61027-146-2 (pbk.)
ISBN 978-1-61027-147-9 (eBook)

Publisher's Cataloging-in-Publication

Friedman, Lawrence.

    The book club murder / Lawrence Friedman.

        p. cm.

    Series: *The Frank May Chronicles* (#5)

    ISBN: 978-1-61027-146-2 (pbk.)

1. Lawyers—California—Fiction. 2. San Mateo (Cal.)—Fiction. 3. May, Frank (Fictitious character)—Fiction. I. Friedman, Lawrence. II. Title. III. Series.

PS357.F768 2012   814.'3'5663—dc22

20120154799

for Leah, Jane, Amy, Sarah,
David, Lucy, and Irene

THE
BOOK CLUB
MURDER

1

It was a lucky break—a fluke—that saved my wife, Celia, from a truly awful situation. If she hadn't had a migraine headache—real or imagined—she might have been a suspect in a murder case.

Before I explain, let me briefly introduce myself, to those of you who don't know me. My name is Frank May. I'm 44 years old, I live in San Mateo, California, and I'm a member of the California bar. I practice law—I'm what is known as a solo practitioner. In other words, I don't have any partners. My office is in downtown San Mateo, about a ten-minute drive from my home. If you're not familiar with northern California, I should explain that San Mateo is a suburb of San Francisco. San Francisco is at the tip of a peninsula; the peninsula itself juts out between San Francisco Bay and the Pacific Ocean. If you drive south, along the bay, pretty soon you get to San Mateo. It's a nice place to live. Tourists never go there, of course. They flock to San Francisco, but they never wander down to my habitat. I like San Mateo, but there's nothing a tourist would especially want to see. There's nothing particular *to* see.

I should also add that I'm a married man. My wife's name is Celia. I have two teenage daughters. They go to a local high school. Celia is a high school teacher herself. She teaches in a different high school, across the Bay, somewhere in a vast suburban wasteland. Teaching adolescents should qualify a person for hazardous duty pay. Celia seems to bear it fairly well. Anyway, two incomes are better than one.

Celia belongs to a book club. Thousands of women seem to belong to book clubs. All of the members of Celia's club are women. I think that's typical. Men don't join book clubs, for some reason. Not the men I know, anyway. Husbands and boyfriends never go to Celia's book club. They're not wanted, I suppose. Or they're not interested. Whatever. In any event, Celia's group meets every three weeks, usually on Wednesday nights. There are ten women in the group, but they don't all show up for all of the meetings. They spend half the evening discussing some book; the rest of the evening, it seems to me, they argue about which book to read next. They also indulge in coffee and cake, unless they're on a diet, which most of them are, in which case fruit and raw carrots replace the cake. And then they gossip, I suppose. That's the agenda. A murder isn't part of the plan. But still, murder is exactly what happened.

The books they read are mostly modern novels. I think they've read novels by Philip Roth, and other people whose names escape me. The most recent book chosen was *The Chickpea Harvest*, a book by a young woman named Griselda Grisby, a thinly disguised autobiography. Celia loathed the book. She found it grim and unpleasant.

The critics, on the other hand, loved it. When it was published, it got a rave review in the *New York Times* book review section. "It combines intimacy and valor," the review said, "it plumbs the depths." I have no idea what it means to combine intimacy and valor. Celia had no idea either. And she definitely had no use for the kind of depths this book was plumbing.

"The main character is a woman named Dorothea," Celia told me. "She gets raped by her uncle. Marcus was his name. She was 15 at the time. He makes a sex slave out of her for five years. This takes place in Cleveland, Ohio: that's where Grisby was from."

"Did she have a real-life uncle?"

"Who knows? Anyway, in the book, Dorothea definitely has this uncle. But no father. She had no idea who her father was. Her mother was a famous artist, but then she became a drug addict, and she kills herself in the second chapter. The uncle, the rapist uncle, that was her mother's brother. They had a sex thing going too. I mean, he was sleeping with both of them, mother and daughter. His sister and his niece."

"With both of them? In the same bed?"

"Really, Frank. No. You know that's not what I meant. I meant, he'd be with one woman, then with the other one. With his sister, it was a romance thing. With the niece, well, I told you, he raped her. It's in the book. In graphic detail. And then later, we find out, he was actually her father, as well as her uncle—and he was bisexual anyway. He was sleeping with a nephew too. I suppose there are such people, but I don't need to read about them. The book was, I think, simply revolting. I couldn't stand it."

"Who on earth picked it?"

"I think it was Grace's idea. She has sex on the brain. But really, Frank, it got these glowing reviews. I think it won some sort of prize."

"Maybe the author was just trying to shock people. Shock sells books, I suppose."

"People are hard to shock nowadays," Celia said. She said it in a voice that seemed suffused with spiritual exhaustion. Maybe it comes from teaching high school students. Try shocking *them.*

"These books you read, they never have a real plot," I said.

"Oh, Frank, don't show your ignorance. There's definitely a plot. A lot happens in the book. Too much, maybe. Dorothea escapes from her uncle, there's this older woman, a professor of philosophy, and she helps Dorothea get away. Then the two women become lovers. They buy a cabin in Montana, near a town named Bozeman... there's something later about a moose. Frank, I don't think you heard a word I said. Aren't you interested?"

"She was sleeping with a moose?"

"I knew you weren't listening. No, nobody slept with a moose."

"So why did you bring up the moose?"

"It was symbolic," she said. "They're in the cabin, they're making love, and then they look out the window, and they see a moose in the moonlight. A huge moose, with antlers, very majestic. Then later on, the book keeps referring to this moose. You know, how strong it was, how primitive, and so on. It's a symbol of something. Then the woman, the lover— her name was Miranda—she develops cancer. At the end, she dies...."

"Where do the chickpeas come in?"

"I forget. It's in there somewhere. Something or other is compared to a chickpea harvest. Really, Frank, don't press me."

"And you enjoyed this book?"

"I said I didn't. It was ghastly. I can't imagine why people write such things. It's like going around naked. The woman who wrote the book.... I read in the paper that a lot of this was taken from her actual life."

"Including the moose?"

"Oh, Frank, don't act like a boor."

We dropped the subject for a while. In the evening, before going to bed, we watched the local news-hour. It's a ritual with us. Later, after brushing my teeth, I asked Celia whether she intended to go to the meeting, since she hated the book so much.

"I feel I have to. It's at Millie's house. She and her husband—they have issues. I'll tell you about it some time. I almost feel sorry for her. Or him. Anyway, I'll go, but I just dread what the discussion will be like. There's so much sex in the book, it's all over the place, in excruciating detail; and that will inspire Grace to talk about her own sex life, which she does at the drop of a hat. I can't stand it when she goes on as if she's the most desirable woman in the world, and men are not only dying to have her, they *do* have her, one after another. Or more than one at a time, I mean, really, she's capable of anything. Or at least of *saying* anything."

Grace's sex life, to be honest, struck me as probably more interesting than the book. I had met Grace, and formed my own opinion; but that comes later. Anyway, I refrained from asking anything else.

The meeting was supposed to be held at Millie's house. That would be Millie Unger. She lived with her husband,

Gerald, down the block from us, about five houses away. Her house looked very much like ours. In fact, all the houses on the block look very much like ours. On the outside, anyway.

Our conversation took place the night before the meeting, on a Tuesday in the fall, after the kids were back in school. On the actual day of the book club, however—which was Wednesday—Celia came home from work with a splitting headache. I heard her talking on the phone: "You girls will have to do without me. I've got a terrible migraine, things are flashing in front of my eyes. I'm going right to bed."

At the time, I wondered whether the headache was real... or just an excuse not to go. But in fact, she really had a headache—Celia doesn't like to lie—and I saw her taking painkillers; but I honestly think it was maybe not as severe as she made out. I think she was just as glad not to go. I'm eternally grateful. This was what New Age people call karma, I suppose. How many times since then have I blessed the fates that kept her away! It was like missing a plane connection, and the plane crashes on takeoff and everybody is killed.

Because, you see, the most amazing thing happened at that book club meeting. Millie's husband, Gerald, came home at about 8:30, said hello everybody, or something like that, and excused himself. The women were in the living room, talking. Then he went to the back of the house. That's what husbands are supposed to do on book club nights.

By 10:30 or so, all the women had gone home. Millie went into her bedroom, and there was Gerald, stone cold dead. And not just dead, but murdered. As I later found out, somebody had hit him over the head, at around 9:30, knocked him unconscious, and then smothered him to death. Millie started screaming (she said), and then she called an ambulance, and also the police. The ambulance was pointless, of course. The man was dead. I don't know why she called the ambulance. I suppose she thought it was the thing to do. In the movies, they always call an ambulance, even when somebody is dead. And Gerald was most definitely dead.

2

I heard about these events second-hand, of course. Mostly from Millie herself; after all, she was the only one who actually saw the body.

"Thank God you didn't go," I said to Celia. "Now we don't have to be involved. At least not directly."

"Why are you hedging, Frank? What do you mean, 'not directly'?"

"Well, dear, I have to tell you, Gerald was a client of mine. I helped him with his will, and some other stuff... and I suppose Millie, well, she'll want me to handle the estate, now that he's dead."

Celia found this intriguing. "His will? I heard from somebody that Gerald had quite a bit of money. Somebody else thought he was broke; but I imagine that can't be true. He was in some kind of business. Computers or software or something. Anyway, doesn't it all go to Millie? Under the will?"

"Really, Celia, I don't care to say. And I have no idea how much money he had. How would I know?"

"Frank, I'm your wife. I'm not asking for some sort of dark secret. Who am I going to tell, anyway?"

The other women, I thought. But I kept this to myself. I said, "honestly, Celia, there was nothing special about his will. As much as I remember. I write a lot of wills, you can't expect me to remember what's in them. I suppose I'd remember, if there was something really strange and unusual about what he did. Must have left everything to his wife, or something like that. Did he have children? I don't remember. Maybe he had a sister, or was I thinking of somebody else?"

"I was wondering about motive," she said. "Why would anybody want to kill Gerald? Anyway, it's just appalling, the whole thing. To think, my own book club...."

Indeed. Every so often, the meeting is at our house; I help Celia buy the food, but otherwise, I'm expected to make myself scarce. Nobody has been killed or injured at our house, although Victoria, one of the members, did run over a neighbor's cat while backing out of the driveway. That's the closest it's come to violent crime.

"I suppose that's the end of this book group," I said.

"Well, we're certainly not going to go on as if nothing happened," she said. "You know, they actually scheduled the next meeting, it was going to be at Victoria's, on a Wednesday, as usual. That was before they all went home and Millie found the body. But now I just don't know. I can't imagine how we could face each other."

She didn't have to say it. I know what she meant. How could they face each other, thinking about the terrible thing that happened, the last time the group got together. Wondering who or what was responsible. Wondering—and this was the most ticklish thing of all—if one of them, one of the group, was guilty of cold-blooded murder.

3

Celia had to go to work, of course, the next day. When she came home, she announced that on the way she had picked up some takeout food, at one of our favorite Chinese restaurants. "I just don't feel like cooking," she said. The kids—my two teenage girls—were off somewhere anyway. Cooking a whole meal just for a husband is clearly a waste of time. The way to a man's heart may be through his stomach, but after twenty years, it's either a well-worn path, or is so overgrown with weeds that it's barely visible.

Not that I minded: I don't insist on a home-cooked meal. I'm not that kind of a husband. Anyway, I like Chinese food. I also like Celia. She has a full-time job, she brings in an income, so she's entitled to pick up shrimp fried rice and kung pao chicken, if that's the way she feels. She certainly doesn't have to struggle with something exotic from the Julia Child cookbook, or anything that needs to be marinated for twenty-four hours, and requires all sorts of weird ingredients. And if she did go to all that trouble, would I actually like the dish, when all is said and done? Not bloody likely. Or she might take it into her head to prepare something disgustingly healthy, like cauliflower.

Celia was also entitled to be tired after a long day at her high school where she confronted, day after day, row after row of sullen adolescents. No doubt she was in fact extremely tired; but the minute she got home, instead of collapsing on the sofa, she made a beeline for the telephone. And after we gobbled down the food—which was delicious—she could hardly wait to get to the phone again. And again. Talking to the women, naturally, about the murder.

Those phone calls took up most of the evening. I read a book and tried to watch television; but there was nothing on that really interested me, although I did find myself intrigued by a reality show about a man who had four wives. He was part of some sort of sect. The wives, all of whom were fat, claimed they got along wonderfully, and that, together with the eleven children, they were one big happy family. Somehow I doubted it. The man had the wives in separate flatlets, in one big house; and he went from flatlet to flatlet, depending on what night it was. You had to admire his stamina, if nothing else.

When it was finally too late for more phone calls, and we were getting ready for bed, I asked Celia, quite gently, what she found out from all of these phone calls.

"Not much," she said. "It's quite a mystery."

"The meeting," I said, "was everybody there?"

"Not everybody. Millie of course: it was at her house. Grace, she always comes. Henrietta. Victoria Bessemer. Sylvia, and Phyllis. Oh yes, Bernadette. Seven women... there's ten of us, actually; but not everybody shows up all the time. I didn't go, as you know. Neither did Samantha, she was out of town. I don't know about Christine... but she wasn't there.... Oh yes, once in a while, there's Tanya; she's not part of the regular group. She's Henrietta's granddaughter and lives with her. She drives Henrietta and picks her up. Sometimes she stays, if she's interested in the book. She did last time, when we met at Samantha's. But she wasn't there this time. No, it was only the seven."

Seven women. I think I had met them all, one time or another. But they weren't exactly dear friends of mine. I had more to do with some than with others. To tell you the truth, sometimes I mixed them up in my mind.

Usually, I fall asleep around 10:30. Celia stays up for a while, reading. This evening was different. I felt wide awake. I wanted to talk. And Celia did, too. It's not every day that a murder takes place down the block. And under these peculiar circumstances.

"Tell me what happened," I said. "All I know is the bare bones. You were on the phone all night. You said you didn't find out very much. Didn't anybody say something that, well, something that was interesting?"

"Nobody. Really, Frank, it's a nightmare. You don't actually think... that one of the women—oh, it's impossible."

"I don't know them all that well," I said, "so I can't say whether it's impossible or not. After all, somebody did kill the guy. I suppose it could have been a burglar, or something like that."

"Do you really think so?"

I had to admit I didn't. "It doesn't seem likely. I mean, burglars don't usually go into houses that are all lit up like a Christmas tree, with cars in the driveway, and there's obviously something going on inside."

"What are you saying, Frank?"

"I'm saying, the chances are, it was one of the women," I said.

"But... I just can't imagine that. It's so... well, ridiculous. I mean, I could imagine Samantha killing somebody; but she wasn't there."

"Samantha?" I had only a vague memory of that woman. "Oh, Frank," Celia said. "You never pay attention. Men only notice women if they have big breasts, or no breasts, or something unusual. Really. You've seen Samantha dozens of times."

"Is she the fat one? The one with the mole?"

"Is that all you can say about her? She's an orthodontist, and she's quite successful. She has an office in Saratoga. But they say she almost killed her first husband, and he had to get a restraining order, which was very embarrassing for him."

I vaguely remembered the story. I asked Celia whether she thought Samantha could have driven up, secretly, from Saratoga, and gotten rid of Gerald, who, after all, was not the subject of a restraining order.

"Except that she was in Boston," Celia said. "She just got back this morning. I spoke to her for *hours*. She wanted to know every last detail. Of course, I didn't have much to contribute. Christine wasn't there either. She had the flu."

Celia was almost too excited to sleep. I woke up, as usual, to go to the bathroom in the middle of the night; and Celia was in the living room, reading a book, which was most unusual at 4:00 a.m. I imagine there's nothing like a murder to disturb your sleep.

Celia woke up late. There was no school that day; it was some sort of school holiday. For all I know, it was Millard Fillmore's birthday—or Admission Day, the day California became a state. I happen to be glad California is part of the Union, but why your children have to celebrate by staying home and making trouble is beyond me.

We had coffee, and of course continued talking about the "Event at the Book Club."

"Frank," she said. "The thing you said. About burglars. I mean, about it not being burglars. I can't get that out of my mind. You really think it's one of the women?"

"Well, I'm not a detective. But... it really looks that way, doesn't it? But which one? You know them so much better than I do. I mean, you never can tell, honey, can you? I mean, what people are really like."

"Well, it couldn't be Henrietta, could it? She's 82 years old."

"Don't be an ageist, Celia. She's quite lively, isn't she, for her age?"

"She is. No question. Makes you wonder what she was like when she was young. She's got a husband, I mean, a current husband. I think there were others. The current husband, I don't really know him. People say he has advanced Alzheimer's, he's basically a vegetable. He's in some kind of home. She lives with her granddaughter, Tanya. Maybe I told you that already. Tanya isn't married, as far as I know. I get the impression her parents are dead. She comes to the meetings sometimes. I told you that Henrietta doesn't drive at night anymore, she goes to the grocery or whatever during the daytime, but she doesn't do highways, and her eyesight isn't good enough for driving in the dark.... Anyway, she complains about cataracts; so Tanya pitches in; she drives Henrietta, and she picks her up."

"Was she there the night that Gerald, uh, died?"

"No. She dropped Henrietta off and picked her up later. Henrietta called her on her cell phone, and she came around. But she never went in the house."

"And Grace... Grace was there, wasn't she?"

"Oh, was she ever," Celia said. "I can't stand her, really. She's the one that's always talking about sex. And always making trouble, if you ask me. She says she loves the group, but she isn't satisfied. It's not enough, she says, just talking about books. She wants us to 'bond,' she says; she wants us to become 'confidantes.' It's not like I'm against 'confidantes,' but with Grace? No thank you! Let's say I just don't want it. I'm happy just to talk about the book, whether we liked it, and what it was all about; but she keeps bringing up this 'confidante' issue. She wants everybody to tell everything about their sex lives."

I was glad that Grace did not prevail. I certainly don't want Celia to talk about her own personal sex life. Which is (I hope) exactly the same as mine. Wild horses couldn't get me to talk about that subject in front of an audience. Even an audience of two. People think men like to boast about their sex lives, but I think that's true mostly for professional basketball players, rock stars, and football studs. Married men, no.

"Did Grace know Gerald well?"

"Not that I know of," Celia said. "Wouldn't that be something, though, if she turned out to be... well, a violent person. But she's capable of anything. I don't know why we put up with her. She's a menace."

Celia is rarely so negative about people. Grace obviously irked her. She went on: "She's 50, if she's a day, but God forbid you should ask her. She dresses like... I don't know what.... Miniskirts, that sort of thing. Cleavage. Too much makeup. She's been divorced three times. Claims to have all kinds of men. When she's not talking about sex, it's about... whatever.

Maybe bonding. Half the time, I have the feeling she never even read the book; she couldn't be bothered. When she does talk about it, she always ties it in to sex. She has sex on the brain. She wants us to be like sorority girls, telling all our secrets, as if we were dating men all the time, or... as if we are like those women in *Sex and the City*."

"Can't you get rid of her? Do the others like her?"

"They don't."

"How did she ever get in the group? I don't picture her as the literary type."

"Frank, don't you remember? She used to live across the street, with one of her husbands, that's how she got in. Or maybe through Millie. Now she's living in a condo some-where.... I think she's had a facelift, too, she's just the type."

"Well, who in the group do you *like*, honey? Why do you go?"

"I do like some of the women. Let me see, of the ones who were there... there's Victoria Bessemer. She's the one I know the least. She's a friend of Grace, she's the youngest, and she's quite beautiful, dark, you know, sort of Latin-looking. I love her hair, the way she wears it. She isn't married. Divorced I think, but I'm not sure. Really, it's amazing how many of these women are divorced. I'm an exception, actually... the rest of them, somehow they never found Mr. Right. Or maybe there *is* no Mr. Right. Just you, Frank, and you're taken."

"You were talking about Victoria, not about me," I said. But I was pleased to hear Celia call me Mr. Right. Right for her at least. I'm in my 40's, slightly overweight, and my hairline is receding. No young woman on the make would consider me Mr. Right. In the body department, anyway. Maybe they could love me for my soul.

Celia went on: "Well, you know what women are like, Frank. We ramble all the time.... Anyway, Victoria: she lives in San Francisco, but she rarely misses a meeting. She used to live down here. She's very close to Grace. It's surprising: they're not a bit alike. Somebody said they were lovers, once upon a time, but really, I don't know. Nowadays, people see lesbians everywhere, any woman who doesn't have a husband or a boyfriend, and even some of those. Frankly, I don't believe a word of it. I mean, about Victoria. Maybe they're cousins. That could be it. There's some relationship there."

"And Victoria," I asked, "is she a likely candidate?"

"Candidate?"

"I mean, could she be the one who... did Gerald in?"

"Oh Frank, it's preposterous."

"But it had to be *somebody*," I said. "The fact is, he's extremely dead. And extremely murdered. Who else is there? How about Sylvia?"

"Sylvia.... I don't see her as a killer.... I like her, but I don't know her all that well. I don't know who suggested her; she doesn't live around here. She's the next youngest. Her father's a professor, she's a lawyer.... She works for a start-up company, something technical. She's engaged, to some billionaire I think... somebody in Silicon Valley. There's all sorts of stories. I've never met him. He's older than she is, well, not terribly old, but old enough. They say he's from India or someplace like that. I think maybe he's a Muslim, but maybe not. Maybe a Hindu. Or he could be a Christian for all I know."

I said: "If he's a Muslim, maybe he has three other wives, and Sylvia will be number four." I kept thinking of the program I had watched about the man with multiple wives, right here in the USA. I couldn't picture Sylvia living with all the other women in some sort of compound. I liked Sylvia, by the way. I found her interesting and attractive. The few times I met her, that is.

Celia said: "Sylvia seems very competent. She's one of the few people I know who could handle a tough situation. Not that I really think of this as a tough situation. I mean, if she had found Gerald dead, she'd know exactly what to do. Call 911 or whatever. She's very efficient. I like her, but she's got a very sharp tongue. You should hear her at the meetings. And she never, never likes the book. She's always critical. I think it's all that law school training. That's what does it."

"How about me?" I said. "I went to law school. Am I always critical? I don't think so."

"Oh, you're different, Frank. Don't let's get off the subject. Who have I left out? Oh, yes: Phyllis. Well, you know her, she lives down the block. You remember, she came by once, she was collecting money for some disease. I think it was a disease. And I left out Bernadette. She's my age, more or less. She's overweight, and she's always on a diet—she never touches the cake, but who is she fooling? She must be gobbling it all down secretly."

"Let's rule her out," I said. "Fat people don't kill."

"Oh, Frank, *can't* you be serious? For all I know, Bernadette is a ruthless killer—aren't some gangsters overweight? They are in the movies. Anyway, she's Sylvia's cousin, I think: that's why she's a member. She lives in Los Gatos, she commutes. She seems quite sensible. I like her. I don't know much about her family. There's a husband or something. That's all. That's the seven of them."

Seven women. I went over the list of women in my mind. I couldn't help wondering which one of them murdered Gerald. If any of them did. It seemed so incredible. Celia must have been reading my mind. "Frank," she said, "I know what you're thinking. How unlikely it all is. Really, I know those women. They have their faults, but they aren't murderers, for God's sake. Even Grace. I keep going over it, again and again; and I can't help thinking it had to be somebody from the outside."

"A burglar, you mean?"

"Whatever. It's just not possible, that one of us did this. We're a book group. Women... you know women aren't violent.... Statistically, anyway. And I keep thinking, good Lord, what if I had gone, what if I had been there? The police, the questions... it would be an absolute nightmare."

"I'm glad you didn't go," I said. "If you *had* gone, you'd be my number one suspect," and I gave her an affectionate poke in the ribs. But she was in no mood for humor. She said: "Stop it, Frank. It's not funny."

She was right. This was no laughing matter. And she was also right that murder is a job for men, not women. When women kill, they mostly kill abusive boyfriends or husbands. I learned about this in law school. The battered woman syndrome. I'm not sure I remember it correctly. I do recall the legal issue; it had something to do with self-defense. Say a man has been beating his girlfriend, he knocked out her two front teeth. He's a drunken and abusive male, a real horror, and wildly jealous on top of that. She's desperate, she feels trapped. So she waits until he passes out, snoring in a drunken stupor, and then she slits his throat. Can she claim self-defense? Classically, no: you had to be in actual, imminent danger, and a sleeping drunk is not what you call imminent. But the modern approach is to let her make this defense.

I didn't think Gerald was abusive. He didn't seem the type. But then again, one never knows. And the women? Book club women, just ordinary women, suburban women sitting around having a conversation, cake and coffee, talking about their lives, their diets, the local gossip. Oh, yes, talking about the book, too; at least at the beginning of the session. I found it hard to imagine Millie's house, and the book club, as the setting for a murder. Still, stranger things have happened. At least, thank God, Celia had an airtight alibi. Me.

4

I'm not fond of funerals. Some people are. They actually enjoy them. There is no taste so weird that you can't find some people, among the billions on this planet, who share that taste. If you need proof, just browse the web. That's proof positive. Anybody can find soul mates—whether it's people who collect old bottles, or Samoan postage stamps or anything else under the sun; you can find jihadists and anarchists; you can find people who are sexually aroused by horses, pigs, maybe even ostriches. Pregnant ostriches.

Maybe funerals are not such a weird taste. I think many old people do like funerals. They have nothing better to do. A funeral fills up the day. And it gives them what we might call survivors' joy—the opposite of survivors' guilt. They think: I outlived that creep! He's gone, and I'm not! I'm looking at his coffin and he'll never look at mine.

Maybe all this is unfair. Old people lose so many friends and relatives. They have to go to an awful lot of funerals. Young people go to more weddings. Or used to, before they decided there was no point getting married.

I myself have to go to funerals at times. A good part of my practice consists of handling estates. There's no real money in drafting wills. (Trusts are another story.) The money comes when a client has the decency to die. If I'm lucky I get to handle the estate. I mention all this as a kind of somber prologue to the fact that I felt obliged to trudge off to the funeral of Gerald Unger. He was, after all, sort of a client.

The funeral service was in a church in downtown Palo Alto. I arrived early, and signed the book—very important—to prove that I was there. But I was taking no chances. I looked around for Millie, but I didn't see her. The "immediate family," I was told, "was with the coffin in a side chapel." People were standing about in the lobby of the church. Celia was with me, and she pointed out various people. I noticed a sullen looking adolescent, wearing a somewhat scruffy jacket over his blue jeans. He was as skinny as a rail, and kept craning his neck and fidgeting. He had long, black hair; it looked distinctly greasy. He had a prominent Adam's apple and a very unattractive and receding chin. Celia told me that was Justin, Millie's son.

After a while, we all took our seats; the coffin was carried in, and Millie and Gerald's family trooped into the church. At least I assume this was Gerald's family. There were two stout women, more or less middle-aged, with sour looks on their faces; and a very old man, who tottered in by their side, with white hair and a vacant look. This (I was told) was some ancient uncle, well over 90, who came with the two stout women, his nieces (Gerald's sisters). I never quite caught the name of the place they came from.

Millie looked appropriately solemn. She was a woman of about 50 or so. She was thin, like her son, with a somewhat pointy nose; but her chin was quite prominent. If Justin was her son, he must have his father's chin. Or his father's no-chin. Millie had very glossy black hair, no doubt dyed. As I recall, she had a rather annoying, nasal voice. She was dressed in black, of course.

I won't bore you with details of the service. The women from the book club were all there in the audience. One or two women who were not in the book club cried ostentatiously during the service. The reverend said nice things about Gerald. Whether he actually knew Gerald was far from clear; probably not.

I would have gone to the cemetery, but Celia insisted on going home. Not that I was anxious to go, but unlike funerals I do like cemeteries. I find them fascinating. I can wander about, reading headstones, looking at inscriptions, figuring out who lived a long time, and who died young. I like to look at family mausoleums, with their elaborate celebrations of death; or maybe it's the celebration of wealth and pomposity, whatever. I particularly like the oldest graves, the sentimental ones, with weeping willows etched on them. I like neat graves with careful headstones and fresh flowers, and old and neglected graves, with headstones leaning this way and that.

Celia wants to be cremated. For myself, I rather like the idea of an actual grave, a place, a headstone. Not that anybody would ever come to visit. I can't imagine my children in a cemetery. They would say that it "creeps them out."

5

I thought the funeral would bring a kind of closure, that it would signal the end of any involvement with the murder, though not, of course, with the estate. The estate did have to be tended to. And, in fact, Millie called me a few days later and asked to come see me. "I need to talk about the estate," she said. "Of course," I said. After all, I had drafted Gerald's will. That doesn't guarantee that the draftsman will get to handle the estate (and collect a fee), but it's a big help in that direction.

Estates, as I said, are a big part of my business. They're bread and butter for me. It's not as if I'm a kind of legal vulture, hovering in the sky, on the lookout for carrion; but I do need to make a living. And we all have to die. Other things being equal, it's better to die with a little money, and thus help a lawyer who has a wife and children and a mortgage make a living. The fees are, I think, quite reasonable. The clients do not necessarily agree. Anyway, the state of California has a table of official fees, based on the value of the estate. There's a lot of work to be done for estates. I think I give value for the money.

Millie arrived promptly. She had on a black dress, either as a sign of mourning or because she liked the dress. It doesn't matter. She was carrying a black leather purse, which she wore over her shoulder. Her hair seemed glossier than before—more dye, no doubt. She sat down wearily in front of my desk.

"Thank you for coming to the funeral, Frank," she said. "I appreciated that. It was an awful ordeal."

"I was glad to... pay my respects."

Did she give me a dirty look, because of this shameless platitude—or was I imagining things? She went on. "Did you notice," she said, "Gerald's family, the way they behaved at the funeral? They snubbed me. I tried to be friendly, but no use. It was so unpleasant, Frank, they treated me like a leper. I can't tell you how much it hurt me. At the funeral, of all places. Such bad taste. If I never see them again, it'll be too soon."

I nodded in agreement. Funerals were no place for misbehavior.

"My cousin Eliot was there," she said. "He flew in from New York. I was so touched. He's a partner in some gigantic Wall Street business.... Did you meet him?"

I had to admit I hadn't had the pleasure.

"Eliot is terribly busy. He came all that way, and he hardly knew Gerald. I was so glad he was there. Of course, he had to fly back right away. So many friends came, too. And all of the women were there, the women from the book club. That was really so nice. I felt... a kind of solidarity," she said.

I couldn't help thinking: was the woman who killed him there? Was she sitting in the audience, showing solidarity? Of course I said nothing out loud.

"It was a terrible strain," she said. "And all those people telling me, how sorry they were, and what a loss. Naturally, I'm sorry he's dead. And the whole thing is so sordid. I mean, in my own house, and finding the body, and the police, and all of that. But, to be perfectly honest, it's not really a loss, Frank. Do you think I'm a terrible person?"

"No, of course not," I said.

"Thank you. Sometimes, I do get these feelings of unworthiness. And there was something else, too, something horrible, in the air, if you know what I mean. Because of the way Gerald died. Gerald's sister... do you think that they feel... oh God, I can't even bring myself to say it...."

"Say what, Millie?"

"That they think *I* killed him...."

"Oh, that's ridiculous," I said.

"Well, it is and it isn't. And they're not the only ones. I can't stand the gossip. I know people are talking and gossiping, and it's terribly painful. But what can I do about it, Frank? Nothing, I suppose. I walk down the street, and people are staring at me. Or maybe it's just my imagination. But I can't help feeling, they're saying to themselves, there goes the awful creature who killed her husband."

"Really, Millie," I said. "But people who know you...."

"You think? Anyway, I don't want to dump this on you, Frank. It's not the reason I came. I came to talk about the estate. I suppose you're going to handle it."

"Naturally. If you want me to."

"I don't know any other lawyers." she said. This was not exactly a ringing endorsement, but I let it go. "And I think Gerald consulted you, didn't he?"

"He did. But that was a while ago. And... I don't really know much about his affairs. His assets. His estate. I mean, did Gerald have money?"

"He had some. He used to have more, but he invested it in a start-up company. I told him not to, but he never listened to me...."

"It went bankrupt?"

"No, nothing that drastic. That would have been the best thing, if you ask me. That would be the end of it. No, it's not bankrupt, it just sort of goes along, maybe it even makes a profit, but barely."

"What kind of company?

"Oh, something with computers. Don't ask me. I have no idea. Gerald owns half of it, there's a partner, Peter Sanchez. There's just the two of them, they have a small office somewhere, in Silicon Valley, maybe it's in Sunnyvale. And there's a few other people working there, a secretary or whatever they call them these days.... Tanya works there, too. Henrietta's granddaughter. I have no idea what she does."

"Did this other guy, Peter, did he put up any money?"

"I don't think so. He's young. He knows the technical side of the business. He's from Argentina. Maybe the two of them got a little money, from venture capitalists, I was never clear about that. Gerald had some money he inherited. From an uncle. I think they put it in the company. Really, I don't know. I do know the uncle left him something, and I think that same uncle didn't leave any money to Gerald's sisters, which is one reason why they're so angry at me. Besides thinking that I killed their dear brother."

"Did Gerald ever talk to you about... his estate?"

"No, he didn't. You know, it was a second marriage, for both of us. And after a while, we really lived kind of separate lives. The money part, very definitely; that was completely separate. He had his bank account, I had mine. It was like our sex life, to be brutally honest. He had his and I had mine. We had an arrangement...."

"About sex?"

"Oh, Frank, don't be ridiculous. I mean about money. We didn't argue. He paid some of the bills, and I paid some. After all, I earn a living. Maybe I was bringing in more than Gerald at the end. No, we never discussed money matters. I think he once mentioned it, I don't remember when, it was years ago. I said to him, why don't you go see Frank, he's Celia's husband; that's what he does for a living. And I understand he did talk to you."

"He did. We discussed his will. I drew it up for him, but that was years ago. I didn't see him recently. Still, as far as I know, that's the most recent will. Do you know—I don't suppose you do—whether he went to some other lawyer? More recently? My feelings wouldn't be hurt...."

Not my feelings, of course—just my pocketbook. But I didn't mention that to Millie. If another lawyer had a more recent will, that lawyer would expect to handle the estate. Of course, if I could persuade Millie to ditch that other guy he would have to grit his teeth and put up with the situation. It's happened to me once in a while. You write the will, charging some trivial amount, in the hopes of representing the estate; and then the widow comes in, and says, "Do you mind, I'd like my nephew Phil to handle the estate, he's just passed the bar, and he's been so sweet to me." You feel like killing her, but you smile and say yes.

I told Millie I was required to file the will in probate court, and I asked her formally whether she wanted me to represent the estate. She said yes.

I had a file on Gerald, and in it I had some notes about the will, and a xerox of the will. I didn't want to take time to read it now, but I did note that it named Millie as executor. I talked to her for a while, explaining the duties of an executor, and outlining in general the probate process. "You're sure there's no other lawyer?"

She said: "I don't think so. Besides you, no. But I really don't know."

"What about family? I saw the two sisters, at the funeral; did he have parents?"

"His parents are dead. His mother died last year. Father died a long time ago. The two sisters are witches, horrible women, really.... They live in Phoenix. Both of them are divorced; it doesn't surprise me. He had a brother. I think he died, auto accident. Not sure. Gerald never had much to do with his family."

"I thought there were children.... I saw a young man at the funeral...."

"They're mine, not his. You saw Justin. They're children from my first marriage. Gerald and I never had children. I didn't want any more. I had mine already."

"You have a daughter, too, am I right?"

"Ashley. She's in college. I called her, of course, and told her what had happened. But I also told her not to come to the funeral. It's midterm time, and she can't afford to be away. She hated Gerald anyway."

"So... back to Gerald's family. Was there a quarrel? Some reason why he wasn't close to his family?"

"I don't know. Maybe. He never visited his sisters. One of them, Hilda I think, came through town once. Gerald was downright rude to her. I think it had something to do with the uncle's will. As I said, he left Gerald money and nothing to them; and as for the father's will, maybe it was the other way around, he left Gerald out, or didn't leave him much; or maybe he left the sisters out, who knows. There was some money there, but I think it was Gerald's mother's. Anyway, there was bad blood in the family but he never talked about it."

"If there's no later will," I said, "you'd get most of the estate. Or all of it. I'd have to check to see what the will says; and I'd have to look at the statute. But anyway, this is a community property state, you have certain rights."

She laughed. "Well, I hope so. But maybe I'll get nothing."

"How's that? I don't think so. Even if another will turns up, you won't be left out, you know, because of the community property. Basically, half of everything is yours. Unless you had some sort of agreement, which I assume you didn't."

"No... nothing like that. But I read somewhere, I could forfeit it all."

"Forfeit? What are you talking about?"

"If I killed Gerald. I'd get nothing. Somebody told me that."

I had to admit that was true. That was the law in California. And elsewhere. Perfectly reasonable, too, I suppose. Under California law, if you murdered somebody, you lost your right to inherit from the victim. I assume this was meant to keep people from killing grandma for her money. Or maybe it was just the principle of the thing: if you kill somebody, you don't deserve their money.

Out of sheer politeness, I had to add, "But Millie, are you worried? I know there's a lot of idle gossip, but there's nothing to base it on."

"Oh isn't there? The police think I did it, I just know it. They can't prove anything, but there's this cloud over my head. For one thing, there's the fingerprints."

"Fingerprints?"

"Yes, they're all over the place. After all, Frank, I *live* there; of course there's fingerprints, what did they expect? The cleaning lady comes on Saturday, her name is Anna, she's from Mexico or somewhere; she's no good at all, and she doesn't speak English, but at least she mops the floor, and she wipes everything off, and cleans the windows. But this was

Wednesday, not Saturday. Naturally, Gerald's fingerprints were all over the house, like mine. This doesn't prove anything, but it doesn't disprove anything either. And the wife is always the first one they suspect...."

I felt it best not to comment. "But they must have other suspects, no?"

"I really don't know, Frank. They took the prints of all of the women... and I suppose they'll find them in various places in the house, after all, they *were* there, and I suppose we all used the bathroom, and people went into the kitchen too, helping out with the refreshments.... But, from the way they talked to me, and all of that, I just know they think I killed him. Honestly, Frank, it's a nightmare."

"I'm so sorry Millie."

"Of course, I do have an alibi," she said. "We all have alibis. We were all together, in the living room. Everybody was still there, when... when it happened. It's so ghastly, Frank, while we were chattering away, talking nonsense about some stupid book, an absolutely wretched book—did Celia read it? I hated it. Anyway, we were talking and talking, and meanwhile, somebody was killing Gerald in the back of the house. But of course, the police don't give two pins for my alibi; they just don't believe me."

"I wouldn't worry," I said.

"But I *do* worry; wouldn't you? Everybody tells me I have to have a lawyer. My son Justin keeps saying, mom, you've got to have a lawyer. You don't handle this sort of thing, do you, Frank?"

"I don't, Millie. I can recommend somebody...."

"It's expensive, isn't it?"

"I'm afraid it is."

"I'm really mixed up. There's all these people telling me, get a lawyer. Except Marcia. She's the one who does my hair. She said to me, Millie, why do you want a lawyer? Nobody's accused you of anything. Frank, do you think it would look suspicious, if I hired a lawyer?"

"No, Millie, I don't think so. But to be honest, I don't have any experience with this sort of thing."

"Oh, but you do, Frank. Everybody says so. Don't get all modest on me. I've just about decided I do need a lawyer. Because of the suspicions. They always think it's the wife, don't they? Or the husband. I'm repeating myself, I must sound like a broken record. I know they think we had an argument or something like that. And... honestly, Frank, and this is the terrible part, if they start poking around, investigating, snooping, they're apt to find out all sorts of things."

"Things, Millie? What sort of things?"

"Well," she said, "It wasn't exactly like we were madly in love with each other. If we ever were. Gerald, you knew Gerald, but of course, you knew him in a different capacity. I don't want to badmouth him, he's dead; but, well, he wasn't your loyal adoring husband, if you want to put it that way. He had his little diversions. He and I—we weren't getting along, we hadn't been for years.... And... there was talk of divorce."

"Divorce?"

"Well, we talked about it."

"You said he had, uh, diversions? You mean he had a girl-friend? An affair, or whatever you want to call it?"

"Yes... that's exactly what I meant."

"Was it... somebody you knew, Millie?"

"Well, this is the thing, Frank. Nobody will believe this, but I honestly don't know who it was. To tell the truth, I didn't care. That's the God's truth. We had nothing going, and I didn't care what he did. He could have been screwing a chimpanzee, it wouldn't make any difference to me. We were... further and further apart, to put it mildly. And... the divorce thing... I'm ashamed to say this, Frank, but I went so far as to consult a lawyer."

"Ashamed? Why Millie?"

"Because... I should have come to you, Frank. After all, you're my lawyer, aren't you? I mean, insofar as I have one.... And I know Gerald saw you about the will, and maybe other things, whatever. But I felt embarrassed; I mean, Celia's in the book group, and I thought, this is an awkward situation, and... anyway, I went to see somebody else."

"Could I ask you, who?"

"Well, it was a man named Eduardo Gomez...."

The name meant nothing to me. "Eduardo Gomez? Who recommended him? Where did you get him from?"

"You'll be surprised. I got his name from Peter, Peter Sanchez...."

"Gerald's partner? You consulted Gerald's partner—you weren't getting along with Gerald, and you asked his partner for the name of a divorce lawyer?" I could have added: wasn't that a bit weird?

"Yes, I asked Peter.... Don't ask me a bunch of questions, Frank. It's not relevant. Peter is a good friend. I know, he's Gerald's business partner, but I've gotten to know him; and we... uh, talked. About the situation. Gerald's personal life, it doesn't concern him. Eduardo is Peter's cousin. They both come from Argentina originally. Eduardo went to law school here, at Hastings. I talked to Eduardo a few times, you know, about the divorce, money matters, the usual subjects. Eduardo is strictly family law. He doesn't do estates."

"I see. Don't worry, Millie," I said. "I've done some divorces, but if it's at all complicated, I refer it out to other lawyers. I'm sure this Eduardo is OK."

"What concerns me," she said, "is the way the situation looks. I mean, we were thinking of divorce, so that means, we weren't getting along... they suspect me anyway, and that makes it worse, doesn't it? The estranged wife. She hated him, and so on. But really, Frank... how could I have done it? I mean with all those women in the house, it would be completely crazy."

"Could somebody have gotten in?

"I don't know.... It doesn't seem likely. You know our house, Frank. It's quite an ordinary house. It's very much like yours. I don't mean ordinary in a bad sense, don't get me wrong. Anyway, you know the layout. You come in, and the living room is to the right, and a small kitchen to the left, and a hallway to the back of the house. There's a bedroom and a bathroom, and then the hallway turns, and the back of the house is... well, the house is more or less L-shaped. In the back, there's two more bedrooms, and another bathroom.

Gerald's body was in the spare bedroom—oh God, it's so awful even talking about it. There's another bathroom, and a laundry room, and there's a door to the outside, leading from the laundry room. But it was locked. And all the windows were locked from the inside. I suppose I could have hired some sort of hitman, and given him the key. The back door key. You read about such things, you know, hiring somebody to be a killer. Or it could have been a burglar."

"A burglar? How would a burglar get in?"

"Frank, how would I know? How do they get in anywhere? They know how, I suppose. That's what burglars do."

"I have to tell you, Millie, burglars don't like houses full of people," I said. "Breaking into your house would be the last thing a burglar would do. Lights blazing in the house, and a dozen cars out in front. But I suppose it's possible.... And hiring a hitman... you didn't do that, so that's nothing to worry about. They'd have to prove it. I'm sure you have no idea how to do it, anyway, I mean, how to go about hiring somebody to kill your husband. You read in the paper about wives who make these arrangements, but how do they find somebody? Do they go on the internet, or on Craigslist or something? It just seems too ridiculous. I wouldn't worry about it, Millie. And the divorce point, it's actually in your favor."

"How's that, Frank?"

"Well, look at it this way. Why bother to kill the guy? You're going to get a divorce; and nowadays, with no-fault, it's just not a problem. It's not like he could say no, and anyway, he wouldn't have. And there's no custody of children, or anything like that. And the property angle, it just doesn't seem strong enough. So I really don't see a motive."

She seemed to be mulling this over. Then she said: "I guess you're right, Frank. There *is* no motive. OK: I didn't particularly like Gerald and the marriage had gone sour. And by the way, he didn't like me either. But that's not enough to kill somebody.... I just hope the police understand that."

Why did I feel she was holding something back? That she was hiding something from me? It was something in her tone of voice, in her body language. But I shrugged it off. None of my business, anyway. I promised to study the will and get back to her, with more information about the estate, her rights, and how to proceed.

It was a long day for me—phone calls, appointments; and, on top of all that, I had to have dinner with a client. Celia hated those evenings when I skip dinner at home, because I need to tend to some demand of some client, but she always behaves herself. She knows, after all, that business is business. The client that evening was a professor at Stanford, Schuyler Wieck, who taught German literature. Schuyler was middle-aged, slightly bald and pudgy, and extremely pretentious. He had an annoying habit of tilting his head to one side when he talked; and he talked a great deal. I didn't particularly like him, and I didn't want his company for dinner. But a client is a client.

I personally know nothing about German literature, except for big names, like Goethe, which is a very big name, but totally unpronounceable for most Americans. Not that I ever read a word of his masterpiece, *Faust*. First of all, it's in verse; and secondly, it's interminable. I looked at a version of *Faust* once, in translation, read a line or two, and then gave up.

"Oh, I don't do Goethe," Schuyler told me. "My colleague Anneliese does that. She does the classics: Goethe, Schiller, you know. I'm more contemporary. I'm writing a book about German detective novels in the post-war period, I'm exploring the way they express themes of sexuality and violence and how that relates to German tabloid culture."

I nodded and pretended to pay attention. We were at an Italian restaurant in downtown Mountain View. I dug into a plateful of lasagna. His business with me, of course, had nothing to do with German tabloid culture. I did read somewhere about a tabloid that published a picture of the Prince of Wales, naked, taking a shower; they sold zillions of copies. I wondered if Schuyler's scholarly interests required him to read German tabloids. At any rate, his business with me was the estate of his uncle Meinhard. Schuyler, along with two first cousins, were the heirs of Uncle Meinhard, who had lived and died a bachelor. Meinhard had been notoriously stingy, and never parted with a penny, pfennig, or euro during his lifetime, if he could possibly help it. But when he died, rather suddenly, his relatives (who had avoided him for years) found that his house was crammed to the gills with bric-a-brac, including broken Meissen statuettes of shepherdesses, and hideous bits of china and other dishware—along with old clothes, yellowing piles of dirty newspapers, hundreds of copies of *Der Spiegel* and *National Geographic*, also turning yellow; and, to be sure, many examples of German tabloid culture, not to mention pornographic magazines in three languages. Oh yes, and bankbooks that turned out to represent almost a million dollars in deposits. No will was ever found, although the house was thoroughly searched (and fumigated). Schuyler and the cousins were the nearest living relatives, but a huge squabble erupted over who should administer the estate and various other matters. I found the dinner exhausting. Schuyler was a pedantic bore, and his quarrel with his cousins was extremely distasteful. Everybody involved hated everybody else, and I had to tell Schuyler that, as far as the law of estates was concerned, cousin Dietrich's abusive relationship with his ex-wife, not to mention his addiction to alcohol, had nothing to do with his right to inherit, and was legally entirely irrelevant.

6

When I got home, I found Celia in the living room, talking to Mona Gibbs, a friend of hers, and (as it happens) Millie's next door neighbor. They were about the same age and height, though not weight. Celia has always been extremely careful about her weight; Mona seemed to be going in the opposite direction. I shouldn't cast aspersions since I myself am (somewhat) overweight. But Mona was an extreme case. She loved to eat; and we're not talking about broccoli. As a result, Mona was the sort of person who could lose seventy five pounds and never miss it. She also had dyed blonde hair, rather badly done, so that bits of gray and black peeked out at the roots.

They were talking breathlessly about the murder, of course, when I came into the house. Mona smiled at me. "Celia dear," she said, "I need your advice. Or maybe Frank's advice, he's a lawyer. This has to do with mother."

Mona works part-time in a library. She's got a husband, though he seems to be traveling most of the time. I think he's a paint salesman or something along those lines. She has a daughter who goes to community college and studies physical therapy. There was another daughter, who got pregnant and married at some disgracefully young age, but she lives in Bakersfield. Also at home is an old, toothless, and decrepit mother, Emily Finbar. Mona was saying: "As you know, my mother's not as sharp as she used to be. I don't know how much longer we can keep her at home. Bert and I both work and Bert is away a lot, and Brittany is in school all day....

Mother just can't focus, poor dear; I think it's Alzheimer's, but then what can you do? She gets everything all mixed up. She's just not cooking on all four burners, if you know what I mean. It's getting worse... one day we found her on the street, in her nightgown. She was totally confused.... I said, mother, what are you doing out here? She said, am I in Walla Walla Washington? I said, no mother; this is California, this is where you live. She had a brother in Walla Walla, he lived there for years. He had some kind of business, something involving onions. I was told the area there is famous for onions. She was very fond of this brother. I guess for some reason she thought she was visiting him. Poor dear. He died two years ago, but she didn't seem to remember that."

I had met Mona's mother a few times. She did seem a bit dim. I suppose it was dementia coming on. That's everybody's nightmare, of course—becoming demented. I think we'd all like to die fully aware, with all the brain cells firing away. The fire in Mona's mother's brain had been reduced to smoldering embers. I made appropriate noises of sympathy. But I wondered, where was this going? Why were we talking about poor Mrs. Finbar?

"She's definitely losing her grip on reality," Mona said. "Poor mother. And she was such a vigorous woman, in her day. She won prizes for her cherry pie, at bake sales. Anyway... that night, the night Gerald died, mother seemed agitated. Bert and I had gone out, we were invited to dinner by Fran and Mickey Gilhooley, do you know them? They live on the next block, next to California Street. They're dear friends. We hate to leave mother alone, but we thought it was all right. Britanny was due to come home only minutes after we left; well, as it turned out, she didn't get home until midnight, it's a long story.... Anyway, we were at the Gilhooley's, having dessert, and their son came home, you know, Mitchell Gilhooley, the one with red hair, and he had driven by our house, and he said to me, I saw your mother. Where, I said. He said, she was walking around outside the house. And I thought, oh dear. I tried to call Brittany on her cell phone, but she didn't answer.... I got terribly nervous. So we said to the Gilhooleys, we really have to go, it's mother, and they understood, so we rushed on home. But when we got here, there was this tremendous commotion, the police, sirens, an ambulance, and I thought, oh God, it's mother. But it wasn't mother at all. She was sitting in the living room, watching TV."

"So she was fine," Celia said.

"Oh yes... but still: mother can't really manage the TV set, so I knew, somebody must have been there.... And meanwhile, I found out about Gerald, and I was worried, did the sirens and all that upset mother? But of course, she's pretty deaf. Anyway, I said, mother are you all right, and she said oh yes. This nice young man took care of me. I said, what man, but she gave me a blank stare. But don't you see—of course, mother is confused, and she doesn't remember things from one minute to the next, if you ask her what she had for breakfast, and it's been only ten minutes since breakfast, she has no idea. But still...."

We too had blank looks on our faces, so she felt she had to spell out what she meant: "Mother was wandering around outside.... She was in the garden, between the two houses.... Do you see what that means? It was just about that time when Gerald was killed.... and she saw a man, a young man she said; and it must have been that man who brought her into the house. I know she said, a young man, but of course, to mother, anybody under seventy looks young. Anyway, she must have left the front door or the back door open. Now, Frank, who *was* that man?"

"I have no idea."

"And what was he doing there?"

"Not a clue."

"Well, that's the point," she said. "Couldn't it be the man who killed Gerald? He was outside the house by then, and there was poor mother. When I think of the danger she was in, imagine, a murderer!"

"You're jumping to conclusions," I said. "More likely, somebody was passing by, and he sees an old lady, she seems confused, he tries to help her."

"Oh, Frank. Don't be naïve. Do you really think so? Outside the house and in the back? Can you even see that from the street? I don't think so. Of course, she wasn't just in the back. After all, come to think of it, Mitchell Gilhooley saw her, when he drove by.... But how did they get into our house? Mother can't manage that at all. What I want to know is this: should I go to the police?"

I thought a minute. It would be no use telling her not to. She was obviously bound and determined to go to the police. And excited, too. A murder! On our block! I don't think she knew Gerald very well and was hardly in mourning for him. The whole thing was thrilling, and even more thrilling was the idea that she and her family had a part to play in this little drama. Maybe she would even appear on TV! So I gave her the advice she wanted, I said it wouldn't be a bad idea. That's a general tactic for dealing with clients. Tell them what they want to hear, unless they've suggested doing something that they really, really should not do.

So I told her, yes, by all means, do go to the police. But I added a word of caution: "Of course, it doesn't give them much to go on, does it? I mean, if they try to question your mother, I don't mean to be indelicate, but she... she has memory problems, after all."

"Oh, you're right, Frank. That's a problem. But still...."

"Still," I said, "it's information they ought to have. And you should give it to them."

Clearly, I had made Mona's day.

7

I didn't believe for a moment, of course, that somebody killed Gerald, and then acted like a good Samaritan with old Mrs. Finbar. That was just not something I thought must be part of the psychological makeup of killers.

When I got home the next day, Celia was already there, cobbling together a dinner out of leftovers. Dinner gave me a headache; the two girls were squabbling, hardly a rare event, and they greeted the plates of food with cries of "yuck," and in general acted like spoiled brats. I don't want to go into details. Sometimes they can be angels. Especially when they're at somebody else's house, on a sleepover. They save their tantrums for us.

After dinner and the dishes, they fled to their rooms, and Celia and I settled down before the TV set, fully intending to immerse ourselves in that particular mindless narcotic. At about eight o'clock the doorbell rang. Now this is a rare event in suburbia. Unless we've invited people over, it's never anything or anybody we want to confront. I was tempted not to answer. It could be somebody from Jehovah's Witnesses, or a college student begging us to sign a petition—to save sperm whales from extinction, or ban drilling in the Amazon jungle, or whatever. I am perfectly in favor of saving whales, the Amazon jungle, and many other worthwhile things, but I also prefer not to be part of any organized campaign. Life is too short. My life, anyway. Whales have long lives, though. At least I think so.

I also never sign petitions. It's a principle of mine. They can come back and bite you. And, for all I know, I might have valuable clients who would just as soon slaughter every last whale and drill for oil in every inch of the Amazon jungle; and if I signed too many petitions, they might take offense. It's cowardly, but I have to live.

In any event, it was neither Jehovah's Witnesses nor a student eager to save the world from destruction. In fact, it was Grace Norman, the last person I expected to see.

Grace gave me a rather wet kiss on the cheek, and asked if Celia was home. She didn't fool me for a second. She was eager to talk about Gerald's murder. All of the women, of course, were obsessed with this event. No surprise.

Evening television, in short, would have to wait: no great loss. We found ourselves in the living room together, the three of us. Celia made coffee, and offered some leftover pastries, which Grace declined. The topic of conversation was totally obvious—and premeditated, if I may be permitted to use a legal term. Grace had come over to pick our brains, and to share whatever gossip was available.

She was about the same age as Millie, with bleached blond hair that had a somewhat starchy look. She usually wore too much makeup—too much for my taste, at any rate, though I'm hardly an expert. Her eyebrows always looked to me as if they were penciled in. She was full-bodied, verging on a bit of overweight, and she always managed to dress in such a way as to display her more than ample cleavage. She loved bright colors and very short skirts. Too short for her age, if you asked me. She never asked, of course.

Celia was the excuse for coming over: Celia was, after all, in the book group. But, as I might have guessed, I was the real object of attraction. They wanted to discuss the case with me, and not only because I was Celia's husband, but because they imagined I was just the person to figure out what happened and solve our local mystery. Because I'm a lawyer. Because I am rumored to have some sort of skill at this sort of thing. And, of course, because I'm a man. They all expected miracles. All except me.

There was an obligatory moment or two of small talk. Then she came right to the point: "Well, Frank, what do you think? Which one of us killed Gerald?"

"Grace, how on earth should I know? I wasn't there. Celia wasn't there, either, as you know. But *you* were there. Frankly, I don't see how any of you could have done it. Weren't you all in the living room, together, talking about the book?"

"Yes, of course, but if you had to go to the bathroom, you went; I know I did. And so did some of the others."

"Which ones?"

"Frank, dear, I didn't keep track...."

"And how long were people gone, when they went to the bathroom?"

"Frank, how would I know? I mean, I didn't measure the time. They go, and they come back. That's the way it is."

I couldn't help myself from asking, "Did you notice, well, that somebody seemed to be in the bathroom awfully long?"

"No, I didn't. Maybe that happened, but I wasn't paying attention."

I said: "Women always take longer in the bathroom. I mean, longer than men. I don't know why, really. I know they have different plumbing, but still...."

"Oh, Frank, please. Don't be ridiculous. You sound like my ex-husband. Anyway, the whole idea is absurd. Excuse me, I have to go to the bathroom, and meanwhile, let's murder Gerald. I mean, really."

I had to agree: it seemed quite ridiculous. But we all had the same thought: *somebody*, after all had killed him. And who could that be?

"It's so strange, Frank," Grace said. "Of course, it wasn't me. Why should I kill Gerald? I had absolutely no reason to do any such thing. To be honest, I didn't find him very attractive. Of course, he found *me* attractive."

"What do you mean, Grace?"

"What do you think? Men always have sex on their minds. It's the way they're constituted. I don't want to sound narcissistic, but I do have a certain amount of sex appeal. I've been around the block a few times, if you know what I mean. Men have a kind of radar, they can sense when a woman is sexually appealing; and they can sense, too, when a woman, shall we say, takes an interest in the sensual side of life. It gives her a certain kind of erotic attraction. And, to be perfectly honest, I'm that sort of person. I won't claim I'm a great beauty. I'm not ugly, no, and I know how to appeal to men, the things they want. I know I'm not exactly a teenager, but you know, maturity, a mature woman, that has its own appeal. I'm not an old hag, Lord knows. And I'm interested in the sensual side of life. Many women aren't. That's the sad truth."

I grunted something; I suppose she could interpret it as a sign of agreement.

She went on, "It was Millie who killed him, of course. I don't doubt it for a minute. Let's be realistic. None of us would have rushed back and murdered him, it doesn't make sense. And who would want to? But Millie... you know, they weren't getting along; we all knew about their marital troubles, it wasn't exactly a secret. So it has to be her, no? Anyway, we were all talking, that evening, everything seemed normal, we had our coffee, we talked about the book, and then we all went home. I think what happened is this: she went back to their room, and she and Gerald started arguing over something, and she started bitching and complaining, and he was obnoxious, I suppose he was, and maybe he insulted her, called her horrible names, and maybe he even lost his temper and hit her, and she lost her head, she kills him, and then she tries to cover it up, she starts screaming and carrying on, and then she calls the police. That's my theory. It's the only thing that makes sense."

"But, Grace," I said. "The police came right away—that's what I heard; and they have these medical people, too, and they said he had been dead for a while, a hour or more. I don't know how they know these things, but there's a doctor, he examines the body, and they figure out how long the man's been dead."

"Oh, Frank, don't be naïve. They can't be sure, can they? Maybe she waited an hour or so after we all left; let's say we left at 10:00, and she called the police at 11:00.... And then she told them the women had just left, and she went in back and found him. That's her story."

"That wouldn't work, would it, Grace? I mean, they could ask all of you, when did you leave? And then they'd know. It just doesn't make sense."

"Don't be such a lawyer. She killed him. It's obvious. I'm not even blaming her. Believe me, Gerald could be absolutely despicable. I *know*."

She had a look on her face which told me she wanted me to ask her *how* she knew. I fell right into the trap.

"Oh, Frank. I see Celia never tells you *anything*. You didn't know I had an affair with Gerald? It didn't last very long.... It's been over and done with for centuries. Of course, he still wanted me... that was so Gerald. I broke it off, and men can't stand that. Anyway, believe me, I know all about Gerald. And let me tell you, the man was pathetic. Oh, he thought he was God's gift to women; they all do. But if I told you what he was really like... well, I don't want to get vulgar. Anyway, it's no wonder Millie couldn't stand him. She needs a real man. And Gerald.... Not that he didn't like sex, what man doesn't, but I know plenty of men who could have given him lessons."

I tried to act worldly-wise. "And Millie knew about this, about your, uh, relationship with Gerald?"

"Who knows? Or cares. She wouldn't have minded, believe me. There was nothing between them. An empty shell."

I said, meekly, "Gerald must have had some sort of appeal. After all, you didn't *have* to be with him...."

"Oh, Frank. Who knows why people do what they do? Maybe I'm just not choosy. Sometimes I wonder about myself. I rush into things. I'm a woman who needs... well, intimacy. It doesn't have to be a man, does that shock you, Frank? I love women, too. Women make better lovers, I really think so. They're more tender. And more passionate. And more beautiful... don't you think? Frank, let's face it: a penis is simply ugly. Really. It's the honest truth. A woman's body is like a work of art, it really is.... Did you know Victoria and I were lovers, once upon a time?"

No, I didn't know. I guess this was one more thing Celia hadn't bothered telling me. Assuming it was even true. I had the feeling that not everything out of Grace's lips was the gospel truth.

"We're no longer together," she said, blithely pursuing the topic. "Victoria has somebody new. I'm not the least bit jealous. Well, *she* was. Jealous I mean. She was quite a jealous person, but that's another story. Water under the bridge. I never look back. You know, life goes on. I have a new partner now. Partner—that's a funny word, isn't it? As if we're in business. Anyway, his name is Laszlo. He's Hungarian. He does something with computers.... He's extremely romantic, really. He has family in Budapest, and he wants me to go with him. I've never actually been, and I'm dying to go. Of course, he's married. More or less. They're not exactly together. He says his wife is 'irrelevant.' That's the very word he used. I just love it."

Why was she telling me this? I began to squirm. I was feeling somewhat irrelevant, myself.

"He's so hot-blooded, Laszlo," she said. "You know what Hungarians are like. They're different from the rest of the people in Europe. You know, they have a very primitive language, nobody knows where it came from, somewhere in Siberia I think. They're descended from Genghis Khan, the Hungarians, wild horsemen and that sort of thing. They have this veneer of civilization, but underneath, it's all fire and... a kind of savagery. I think that's what attracted me to him. And him to me. I have some of that fire myself. Did you know, I have some Hungarian blood myself: my great grandmother was Hungarian?"

I shook my head, to indicate I hadn't known.

Where was she heading?

She got up, and took her purse. "I really have to go now," she said. "I have a million things to do. But, as I was saying, Laszlo, the work he does; it's some technical thing. Computers. When men talk about these things, I just tune out.... But anyway, he's gotten to know Peter Sanchez. Gerald's business partner. They do some sort of software, I can't keep up with these things. The point is, Laszlo has inside information... about Gerald's company. And, Frank, in the light of all this... well, I wouldn't be surprised if Millie had an accomplice....You know what I'm referring to."

"Frankly, Grace, I don't."

By now she was at the door. She turned and delivered her parting shot: "You don't *know*, Frank? How naïve can you be? How did you ever pass the California bar?"

I wanted to tell her that the California bar—one of the hardest in the country—has questions about torts, and civil procedure, and the American constitution; but nothing at all about sex. And nothing to test how naïve a person might be.

But I never had a chance. She was already gone.

8

It isn't surprising that the murder was topic number one in our neighborhood. Murders don't happen every day. Not in a nice suburban neighborhood. All sorts of wild rumors were going around, apparently. My older daughter told me one of these rumors. The police were about to arrest a young guy, she said, "and Dad, you won't believe this, but he's a high school student, at Paly High, in Palo Alto, and he's been having sex with Millie, and she's old enough to be his mother." She heard this from her friend Francine, who heard it from Tiffany, who heard it from her own mother, who heard it from Felix, the man who owned a beauty salon and cut her hair. This "dude from Paly High" killed Gerald to get him out of the way. "She had him hidden in the house, you know? And when Gerald came home, and found him.... The guy was in a closet, completely naked, because they just had sex, this kid and Millie; and Gerald had an absolute cow when he found the guy, and they had a fight, and the guy slit his throat with a kitchen knife."

Nobody, to be sure, could swear to this, and nobody knew the boy's name, but the ultimate source (they said) was somebody in the know, somebody deep, deep inside the police department. I pointed out how unlikely it was that Millie was having sex with anybody that night; she had a houseful of women—were they supposed to be watching the show?—and Gerald was most definitely not killed with a kitchen knife. But she still thought "there was something to it. Everybody's talking about it."

"Honey, it's a myth. Believe me."

But of course, she didn't believe me. She never does. "What if I told you, Dad, that somebody actually *saw* him? It's totally true. He was seen coming out of the house. That night. There were witnesses."

"Naked? Covered in blood?"

"Dad, don't be prehistoric. No, of course, he wasn't naked. He put on his clothes. And no, he wasn't covered in blood. He must have wiped it off. I told you, somebody saw him. He was wearing a New York Yankees baseball cap."

Well, maybe, and I didn't want to argue, but not a word to this effect appeared in the local papers, which I scanned to see what news they might have. Lots of items about squabbles in the San Mateo city council, and about problems with sewer lines, and the pension fund for city employees. There was police news, yes, about drunk drivers and people who vandalized cars, and an "attempted assault" by an intruder in San Carlos, fortunately interrupted by the woman's husband; but nothing much about the case that had all of us abuzz. Nothing about teenaged lovers. And nothing, certainly, to suggest that the police were on the verge of making an arrest or solving the case of the late Gerald Unger.

The women in the book club, of course, were at the very epicenter of this Great Local Event. This made them celebrities, of a sort, in beauty parlors, supermarkets, and in the offices of local dentists.

"Never wish for something," Phyllis told me. "You might get what you ask for."

She was sitting in my office, on a bright, sunny afternoon (in San Mateo, that's the normal state of affairs). "What is it you wished for, Phyllis?" I asked her.

"Oh, just something exciting. Something to relieve the monotony of life."

Phyllis, of course, was one of the celebrity seven: the women who had been in attendance at the book club meeting the night Gerald died. Phyllis Kramer had asked for an appointment with me, which naturally I agreed to. Now she was sitting in my office. She was a woman in her 40's, with jet black hair, which she wore very short. She dressed quite stylishly, at least to my tastes. She was extremely thin, dieter-thin in fact. She was considered the intellectual of the group. She was married to Sidney Kramer, a certified public account-ant, with an office in Cupertino. I knew Sidney slightly. He had a good reputation, and I once had dealings with him. He helped me unravel the tax affairs of one of my estates. How Phyllis came to marry Sidney was a mystery to me and to everybody. They seemed so unlike. Sidney was bald and chub-by, and looked (to me) decidedly unromantic. But that could be misleading. Even bald, chubby men have erections. Celia told me the marriage was unhappy, at least on Phyllis' side. What Sidney thought nobody bothered to find out.

Phyllis was an amateur poet and writer. She and her hus-band lived in a small house down the block. They had no children. Either they couldn't have children, or they didn't want children. Which one, I have no idea. I would have guessed that Sidney, if he had a say in the matter, would want very much to have children. Bald, chubby men always do.

Phyllis, according to Celia, felt her life was dull and point-less. "I think she'd get rid of him if she had an alternative," Celia said, "but she doesn't. I mean, how would she earn a living? She writes poetry."

I had seen Phyllis at the house, once or twice. I couldn't say I knew her well. I found her somewhat intimidating. Somehow, she made people feel stupid. I don't know if it was intentional. It was the way she responded to whatever you said; or sometimes just the look she gave you. She never actually said: you're stupid, or even implied it. But there was an air about her, a certain haughtiness. A kind of disdain.

I asked her: "What can I do for you, Phyllis?"

"I need some advice. I didn't know where to go. Is this go-ing to cost me a lot of money?"

She said this with a smile, as if it was a joke. But of course she meant it. I said: "Well, I usually charge people, Phyllis. Unless they can't pay. Sidney makes a good living, I think."

"Oh, God, I suppose he does. Sometimes I wish he made less money. Or made money in a more dramatic way. Robbing banks. I wish he led a double life, I really do. Personally, I'd rather die than spend every day, day in and day out, looking at columns and rows of numbers, looking at peoples' account books, filling out tax forms, and whatever else they do. I'd be bored to death."

This was coming very close to home. I felt uncomfortable. What did she think about the sorts of thing *I* mostly did, day in and day out? Drafting documents, talking to people about estate plans. Or maybe she had a more romantic image of lawyers. Maybe she pictured us reducing a jury to tears, or arguing before the United States Supreme Court. But surely she knew better than that. Anyway, I said (and it was hard not to sound annoyed), "I'm not a marriage counselor, Phyllis. Why are you here?"

"Frank, everybody knows, you're an amateur detective... don't deny it... they say you're as sharp as a needle, really...."

I love compliments; but this one I didn't need. I stopped her in midstream: "Phyllis, look: I'm no detective. Forget what you've heard. Really. And why do you need a detective?"

"Because... there's this cloud over our heads.... You know that. Celia's so lucky. I've got to ask her, how do you get a migraine when you need one. I honestly think she *knew* there would be trouble. Some sort of sixth sense, warning her not to go."

"Celia's a wonderful woman," I said, "but sixth sense, no. An honest-to-God migraine, that's all it was."

"Oh, life is so strange. You know, a plane crashes, and you read about people who changed their plans the last minute; and then the ones who got on this plane, the last minute; they thought they were lucky, and instead they're dead. It almost makes you believe in some sort of... karma, or whatever they call it."

Yes, I had to agree, the women were in a weird situation. I couldn't help looking at Phyllis and thinking, was *she* the one who killed Gerald? If her life was so boring and pointless, wouldn't a murder be just the thing to spice it up? And yet, what possible reason could she have to kill Gerald Unger? I said, "It's strange. But there's nothing we can do about it,

Phyllis. I mean, this cloud over your head, everybody's head. I'm sure the police are trying as hard as they can."

"Oh, the police. They're simply stupid. They never solve anything unless it's handed to them on a silver platter. No, something like this requires *insight*, Frank.... Anyway, I want you to listen to me. I've been thinking a lot about this. It's really awful, meeting people on the street, people you know, and they give you that look, and they ask how are you, and so on, but all the time, you know they're thinking, is she the one? Did she kill Gerald?"

"Oh, nobody thinks you did it, Phyllis," I said.

She said, "I hope not. But that's because you know me, Frank. The police... well, never mind. Anyway, I have an idea, and I want to try it out on you. I think Millie killed him. Or rather, she had him killed. Of course, he deserved it. Nobody liked him. I certainly didn't. I couldn't stand him. And... they had no marriage. He was unfaithful, but that's not the worst of it. No wonder Millie was fooling around."

That was news to me. "Millie? Fooling around?"

"Oh, Frank, maybe you're not as sharp as I thought... or doesn't Celia tell you *anything*?" This seemed to be a common theme, and it annoyed me, quite honestly. Celia tells me a lot. Maybe she just doesn't feel like passing along idle gossip.

Phyllis went on. "Oh, it's blatant. I tell you, whenever we get together, if Millie's not around, we talk about it, it's so out in the open. And he's half her age... well, not really; but he's a whole lot younger than she is."

"Who are we talking about?"

"His name is Peter Sanchez... he's from Argentina."

"But... he was Gerald's partner."

She said, "Yes; but so what? That didn't stop them. And now that Gerald's dead, the field is open for them. And, I might add, I suppose, now that Gerald's gone, Peter more or less inherits the business. Along with Millie. Oh, they're quite a pair."

"But... OK, there's a motive, I guess. But... she didn't do it personally, am I right? Is that what you're saying? After all, you were there, Phyllis. How could she have done it? Did she leave the room, say, at 9:30? It's so preposterous...."

"How could I remember? I wasn't paying attention. It doesn't matter, though. You're right. I don't think she did it herself. I think she hired somebody to do it. Isn't that how it's done? I mean, by women like her."

I said: "Really, Phyllis, how would I know? I never hired somebody to commit a murder. And I have no idea how people do these things. You read about it in the newspapers, hired killers, and so on. But in real life?"

She said, "Maybe you go on the web. You can get anything on the web, information, sex, new shoes, reading glasses, whatever. Maybe you can hire somebody to kill your husband."

"You're being sarcastic," I said.

"Only slightly."

"Anyway," I said, "how did this person get in, this killer? And why do it on book club night?"

"I don't know about the timing. But, how he got in—that's easy. The back door."

"Did he have a key?"

"She could give him a key. Or she could leave the door unlocked. Millie might have been very clever about it. And maybe it wasn't a hitman. Maybe it was Peter Sanchez, you know, the lover, they were in this together. They decided, let's get the husband out of the way, then the coast is clear for the two of them."

"And he got in through the back door? Is that what you're saying?" I couldn't help thinking about the old lady next door and the young man, or youngish man, she saw. Maybe that was Peter Sanchez. He slips into the house, kills Gerald, goes outside, and sees an old lady; she's wandering around, and he helps her get back home. That would have been a very nice thing for Peter to do. First, a little murder. Then, to balance it off, a good deed, like a Boy Scout. Be helpful to an old lady.

"Oh, maybe it wasn't the back door," she said. "Maybe they were very clever. Have you ever met Peter?"

"No...."

"Well, I have. He's about the same height as Gerald.... Same general shape, but a lot better-looking. And younger. Anyway, he comes to the front door, comes in, says hi, you can't really see anybody from the living room, I mean, somebody coming in the front door. We hear a noise, and somebody comes in, says hello, as I said, and Millie says, oh, there's Gerald; nobody really looks at him, and he is careful to keep his back to the living room, where we're all sitting, so we all assume it really *is* Gerald, and then he goes into the room at the back of the house, and he kills Gerald...."

"He kills Gerald? But how did Gerald get in, if that was Peter you saw?"

"He didn't get in. He was there all the time, only we didn't know it."

"It's too far-fetched. And how did Peter get out?"

"I don't know. That's what I'm working on.... Wait: he was hiding in the back, you know, in a closet or whatever. OK, everybody's gone; Millie goes back, she finds the body, it's no big surprise of course, but she screams and screams, in case the neighbors are listening, and she calls the police, but meanwhile, she lets Peter out."

"It's too complicated."

"Well, so what? People do complicated things."

"Anyway, why would she want to kill Gerald? If she was in love with this Peter Sanchez, she could get a divorce from Gerald. This isn't the Middle Ages. I think she was actually going to do that...get a divorce, I mean. You don't have to kill your spouse to get rid of him. What's the point? Money? Somehow I doubt it."

"Well, maybe she just plain hated him. Why isn't that a good motive?"

"I suppose it is," I said.

"Anyway, Frank, I have something to bring up," she said. "I've been thinking about this, a lot. And I decided, I'm going to write a novel. I know this sounds terrible, Frank, but my life has been in some sort of rut... just one day after another, nothing happening; and, to be honest, this is the most exciting thing that ever took place in this dreary neighborhood. I've always wanted to be a writer, and this is my chance. I've tried poetry, but what's the point of poetry? Nobody reads poetry. A novel, that's the thing. People still read novels."

I had to agree. After all, the fateful book club was proof of this point. Every month they read a new novel. They find something in the *New York Times Book Review*, some glowing review, and they all go and buy the book. Or they read something by some author they know about. Philip Roth, for example. He seems to write a book a year.

Phyllis went on: "It's going to be a roman à clef, you know, it's fiction, and all the names are changed, but it's based on real people. I'm going to call Millie... Margarita. I'm calling her husband Jeffrey. She kills her husband, just the way I explained it. Oh yes, her lover, he's not going to be a Latin, no, that would be too obvious. I'll make him a Russian. Igor Romanov, that's his name. Grace is in it too; I call her Lucinda."

She went on: "I think I have talent. I majored in English literature. I'm sick of trying to get somewhere with poetry. I had a poem published in a little magazine, just last month. But nobody cares. A novel is something else. I know I can do it."

I sighed inwardly. She seemed so naïve. After all, everybody writes novels. But they don't get published. I hesitated to break this news to Phyllis. Half the people in this country have an unpublished novel in a drawer, or on their computer. My client, Ramona Wintergreen, who inherited a fortune from her great-aunt, wrote a whole series of romance novels. Never published, of course. At least not by a standard publishing house. She made me read one of them, about an eighteenth century pirate, Rodrigo, originally from Spain, who seduced a Carmelite nun, and fled with her to Barbados, where he abandoned her for a beautiful mulatta, who later dies of cholera. The climax was a naval battle, or was it a violent sex scene, or possibly both. I can't remember. It was somewhere in the Caribbean, at any rate. The book was God-awful of course. But I had to read the whole thing, because I was sure Ramona was going to quiz me about it. Which in a way she did. She ended up publishing the book herself, and—as I expected—nobody read it. I think she gave away copies to people in her family.

"It's hard to get published," I said meekly.

"I have connections," she said. "I know somebody who works for a publisher. And Sidney can help me with the financial end.... He has to be good for *something*. But I need some legal advice. Do I need to be incorporated? I read somewhere that people like John Grisham are incorporated."

"No, Phyllis, really, it's not necessary. John Grisham maybe needs it. He sells millions of books."

"And the royalty contracts.... I'll need help with that. I suppose the publishers all want to cheat you out of money, that's what I heard. They write these contracts, and there are things hidden in the fine print. That's where you could be a big help."

"Phyllis my dear, if it got that far: yes, I'd be delighted to help."

Of course, I would be amazed if it ever got that far. But I kept this thought to myself. And Phyllis seemed satisfied. Before she left, she went on and on about the book, how she had sketches of it already, in her head at least, and about her plans, and did I know how much publishers paid in royalties, and what about an advance and so on. I answered her as best I could. I was relieved when she was out the door.

Left to myself, I mulled over the theory Phyllis had advanced, about the murder of Gerald Unger. No, it just didn't seem possible. There had to be a better explanation. But what?

9

It seems as if I was fated to talk to all seven of the women who had been at that last book club session. The Chickpea seven. Grace and Phyllis had already been to see me; the next to come was Bernadette.

She was a middle-aged woman, somewhat overweight. She had gray hair—one of the few women of a certain age, besides Celia, who seemed to refuse to dye their hair. I did not know her terribly well. She lived in Los Gatos, which lies to the south of San Jose, a small, rather upscale town; and she commuted to the meetings. She was, I believe, somebody's cousin—that's how she got into the group. She seemed rather bland and colorless. I knew very little about her family. There was a husband, I suppose. There usually is.

If we assume that all seven women were suspects, and if this was fiction—say, a novel by Agatha Christie—then Bernadette would surely be the killer. That's because she would strike anybody as the least likely of all. The least likely one is always guilty, at least in the mysteries I read. In life, it's usually the opposite. The obvious killer is the actual killer. In a mystery, if there's a dead body, and Joe Somebody is standing over the body with a smoking gun but he claims he didn't do it, he's right—it was somebody else. That's what makes it a good mystery: surprise. In life, that's not the case. Genuine mystery is unusual.

But Agatha in a way got something right. There is no such thing as bland and colorless. That's surface, veneer. That's the way some people present themselves. Or the way they've been trained to behave, or just the way they look. But in fact, everybody has a story. Everybody has an inner something. Not necessarily something deeply dramatic. Not that the mousy housewife is a part-time prostitute, or that the dentist has a cellar full of whips and chains. I mean, everybody has a life, everybody has emotions, desires, habits, thoughts, and dreams. Everybody has a history. The old grandma, pushing a walker; she once had a sex life. Maybe she even had orgasms. Young people today think their generation invented orgasms. I'm sure they're wrong. And the doddering husband might have been quite a guy in his youth; maybe he screwed like a rabbit. Or painted watercolors. Or worked as a longshoreman. Or traveled to Ulan Bator, on the back of a camel. Who knows? Even Bernadette must have something stirring underneath. Not easily visible, but it must be there. So she might just possibly be a killer. Unlikely, I suppose, but the chance is there.

Or did she have a lover? That seemed equally improbable, and yet.... Bernadette and I once had a serious conversation. It was after one of the book club meetings, held in our house. Bernadette told me how sorry she was, that she had no real career. "We have no children; there's no role for me, really. I make Max a good home, but is that enough?"

"Why don't you go back to school, take courses, something like that?"

The idea appealed to her. "I was a good student at college. That was years ago.... I majored in German literature. My mother was half German, and she spoke German to her relatives, so I knew a little German, even before I went to college."

I told her about Schuyler, my client, the German expert. Stanford has night courses, for the general public, and Schuyler was teaching one of those. Bernadette actually enrolled. She loved the course. And she became fast friends with Schuyler, she told me later, thanking me for the tip profusely. Were they more than friends? She seemed to be taking every course he offered; and when Max was busy with whatever it was he did—some sort of marketing, I believe—she and

Schuyler went to movies together. That seemed to go a bit beyond friendship. Was she actually becoming involved with Schuyler? Was it more than movies? Was it, possibly... sex? Of course I was much too discreet to ask.

"I had to see you," she said. I nodded. She was sitting across from me, in my office. She was holding a large brown purse in her hands, as if she depended on it for moral support.

"It's good seeing you, Bernadette. How have you been?"

"Oh, Frank, can you even ask. I can't sleep at night. Poor Gerald.... You don't know how lucky Celia is, not to have been there. It's so dreadful. It's the worst thing that ever happened to me. To think, we were talking away, chattering, about that awful book; and somebody was... doing that thing, killing Gerald. Gerald! And that's why I have to talk to you."

"Sure, Bernadette; I'm happy to talk. What's on your mind?"

"You can give me advice," she said. "Frank, I think people trust you. I certainly do. You're a lawyer. People say, you have a knack for... solving crimes. No, don't protest. I know you're a modest person... and very discreet."

"Yes, I am discreet," I said. "It's part of the job. But the rest of it, no. In a couple of situations, I was lucky: coincidences, or just happenstance. I mean, about solving crimes. Really, Bernadette, I'm the furthest thing there is from a detective. If you think you need somebody, I can refer you to a criminal lawyer, or an investigator. But why don't you just leave this business to the police? They're working on this; that's their job, and I'm sure they'll find out who killed Gerald."

But she broke in, and said, with a real touch of panic in her voice: "Frank, please, listen to me. You don't understand. I told you, this whole thing is such a nightmare...."

"Of course. For all of you."

"But for me, specially," she said. She paused, and said, with a kind of gulp, "For me... because I think I know who killed Gerald."

"You— you know?"

"Frank, listen. I.... I'm a person who pays attention.... I notice things....We were all discussing the book.... and people get very involved. Grace—you know, when she gets started, she goes on and on.... I don't think anybody else noticed, but me...."

"Noticed what, Bernadette?"

"Noticed—that—well, this person was gone at least fifteen minutes. I mean, we all went to the bathroom, but... this was different."

"Who are you talking about?"

"Victoria. It was Victoria. She left us, quietly. She went in the back of the house. They have two bathrooms. But when we're at the house, we only use the front bathroom; the back one, it's off the master bedroom, and, well, we don't need to use it, we use the front bathroom. OK, I... I had to go to the bathroom. I really had to go. I have bladder problems, I've been to the doctor, and he wanted me to take pills, but I'm afraid of pills, Frank. I don't like to take medicine. Anyway, that doesn't matter. But I really had to use the bathroom, and that's why I was wondering, where's Victoria? She went in that direction, toward the bathroom, and she's been gone a long time.... So... finally, I thought, maybe she's not all right, so I went to the door of the bathroom, but the door was open. She wasn't there. Maybe she was in the back bathroom, but I don't think so. Why would she go there? So where was she? Where was she, Frank? She was somewhere in the back of the house...."

"Go on."

"I thought, this is odd. But I didn't make anything of it, at the time. So I went to the bathroom and then back to the living room. And by then, Victoria was there. But she looked funny, out of sorts, you know, somehow strange. I said, Victoria, are you OK? She said, yes, my stomach is a little upset, it's nothing. And we were talking about that dreadful book, about the chickpeas, and I forgot about Victoria and everything. But then later... after all this came out, you know, Gerald getting killed.... Frank, what should I do? Should I go to the police?"

I thought about it. It did seem strange, the circumstances. Victoria; was that possible? And was that fifteen minutes enough time to kill Gerald? The whole thing seemed so peculiar. A woman just gets up from the group, goes to the back of the house, and kills the husband of her hostess? I didn't an-swer for a moment or two. Bernadette put the question to me again: "Frank, did you hear me? Should I tell the police what I know?"

I had no idea. "Maybe not, Bernadette," I said. "I mean, I understand, it looks a bit suspicious; but after all, it isn't much to go on, is it? I take it this took place after Gerald came home."

"Yes it did. It was about the time... oh dear, about the time the police thought—you know what I mean. About the time he died."

"Still," I said, "it's hardly more than a vague suspicion, isn't it? I realize it's unsettling to you. But after all, why should Victoria kill Gerald? I imagine they hardly knew each other."

There was a short, pregnant silence. Then she said: "But you're wrong, Frank. They did know each other."

"You're hinting at something, Bernadette."

"A couple of weeks before, I was shopping, I was at the Stanford shopping center. You know I live in Los Gatos, that's where I shop. But I was visiting a friend in Palo Alto; we were going to have lunch, at the shopping center, besides, there was a big sale at Bloomingdale's... it doesn't matter. My friend had to leave, I thought we'd have lunch, but she had to go home, her mother was sick; so I went into a restaurant, it's called Dragonwick, it's Chinese, and... I saw them there, having lunch—Gerald and Victoria."

"And so, Bernadette? I don't want to seem obtuse, but this is the 21st century; a man can have lunch with a woman, it doesn't mean anything, does it? They were friends, I suppose. Are you suggesting there was something more?"

She said: "Trust me, Frank. I know what you're saying. Of course, that's what I thought too, they're friends, or they just happened to meet. Anyway, they didn't see me. I thought I should go say hello, but... I was sitting at a table, not too far away, and I could see them... and I could tell from body lan-guage, from the way they were talking, I mean, it was awfully intense, Frank. And... I'm ashamed to say, I followed them when they left. They went out to the parking lot. They got into

Gerald's car. I mean, I think it was his car. They went off together. They were having an affair, Frank. I'm sure of it."

"OK, maybe you're right, Bernadette. But... that's no motive either. Maybe they were having an affair, sure. Still, that doesn't mean she killed him. In fact, if they were lovers, that's the opposite of a motive. You don't just up and kill your lover."

"But you do, Frank, if he's unfaithful, or... well, there could be other reasons. Isn't it the case, most murderers are people who know the victims. Disappointed lovers, that happens, doesn't it, Frank? And *somebody* killed him, Frank. I know what people are saying, they're saying it was Millie. I don't believe that. But I understand why they're saying it. You don't just kill a random stranger. That's why, the biggest suspect, it's the wife. The next biggest, well, if Gerald had a lover... who knows, they might have had an argument. She went back to the room where he was, and they had an argument, and... she killed him. Maybe it was an accident."

"It was no accident. Somebody hit him on the head, and then smothered him. You can't do that accidentally."

"All right, Frank. So it wasn't an accident.... That's even worse, isn't it? It means she planned it...."

"I don't see how it could be something she planned. How could she know if Gerald would be home at all?"

She paused to think about this. "You're right, Frank; there's a lot of questions, but still, what was she doing back there? That's why I want your advice. I've got to ask you again: do you think I should talk to the police, or should I keep quiet?"

I asked myself, what would *I* do in her situation? I think I'd do nothing at all. I told this to Bernadette. "After all, Bernadette, as I said, it's really just a suspicion. You haven't got anything concrete to go on. Besides, I'm sure the police are working on the case. Maybe they're on to something. Maybe they'll find some real evidence.... Anyway, I really wouldn't want to have to deal with the police; and I bet you feel the same way."

She got up to go. "You're right, Frank. And I'll follow your advice. But I still think Victoria did it. And how can I look her in the face?"

10

I had no answer to Bernadette's question. How, indeed, could Bernadette look Victoria in the face? Perhaps she didn't have to. I on the other hand did have to look her in the face, as you will soon see.

You know, it almost seemed as if there was a conspiracy—as if the women in the book club had all conspired to come see me, one at a time. What touched it off, no doubt, was the absurd rumor that I was "working on the case," and that I was some sort of gifted amateur detective who could solve cases with the ease of, say, Sherlock Holmes or Miss Marple. Of course nothing could be further from the truth.

Not that I didn't find myself *thinking* about the case, and wondering about it. Who on earth could have killed Gerald? There were three possibilities, so far. First, it could have been Millie. That was based on nothing much except the fact that she was his wife, and that they weren't getting along and perhaps were unfaithful to each other. Second, there was Victoria. That was Bernadette's theory and God knows who else's. It was based on the fact that Victoria stayed too long in the bathroom, or rather that she stayed too long *not* in the bathroom, along with the suspicion that she and Gerald had been lovers. The third theory: the culprit was an unnamed and unknown man, possibly young, someone seen lurking around the outside of the house, and who may or may not have taken Mona's mother home. I was partial to this third explanation. It let the women off the hook. But of course there could be all sorts of explanations for the mysterious stranger. Somebody collecting money for Greenpeace, or Jehovah's Witnesses, for example. To be sure, these people rarely come around at night, and they march right up to the front door.

I suppose there was a fourth theory. The burglar theory. This seemed very unlikely. But then, so were the other three theories.

At any rate, as it happened, I was about to get visits from two out of the three suspects—Millie (again); but first of all Victoria.

Victoria was the youngest and by far the prettiest of the group. Except for Celia, of course; but wives don't count. Wives are both beautiful and not beautiful by definition. Victoria was slim, dark, with a roundish face, very dark eyes, jet black hair, which she wore quite long, and vaguely Latin features. She had a figure that was well developed in certain right places, and modestly proportioned in all the other places. She was, to my taste, always stylishly dressed, although Celia found fault with some of the clothes Victoria wore. I had spoken to Victoria several times, about this and that; and even once about a legal matter; it concerned a parcel of real estate that her mother had owned. Real estate is by nature boring, except to people in the real estate business, most of whom are boring themselves. I suppose it isn't a bore to people who are trying to buy or sell a house. I won't go into the details of this particular real estate problem. It isn't relevant, anyway.

Victoria was single. She lived in San Francisco in a neighborhood near the Castro, filled with young and youngish people who ate sushi and worked for computer companies, advertising agencies, start-ups, and the like, though never for any company that actually made something. Victoria did not work for any company at all. She taught art history at a community college somewhere on the Peninsula, I forget exactly where. Her hobby was watercolors. I had seen some of her work—pale, wispy pictures that vaguely looked like landscapes, or maybe they were supposed to be bodies, one couldn't really tell. She also wrote poetry, like Phyllis. Maybe that's why they were friends, if they were in fact friends.

Once, when we were talking about her mother's real estate, which was why she had come to my office, we somehow wandered off the subject, and she began to discuss poetry. I remember, she asked me, who was my favorite poet? This was a terribly embarrassing question. I felt like telling her: I'm a guy. Guys don't have favorite poets. But I didn't say that. I was ashamed to admit I had no favorite poet at all. Or an unfavorite, for that matter. So I said, Emily Dickinson. This seemed like a safe enough lie. I vaguely remembered reading some poems in school, a million years ago, written by Emily Dickinson, and one in particular that began, hope is the thing with feathers, which I never understood, what on earth could that mean, hope being a thing with feathers. But somehow, the line stuck in my mind, the way things sometimes do. But that's all I know about Emily Dickinson, except she never got married and (I think) never went out of the house, if I remember correctly. Fortunately, Victoria didn't press me further; and when I got home, I checked out Emily Dickinson in Wikipedia, so that, in case of an emergency, I might have something to say.

Victoria, alas, had imbibed some of the same snake-oil as the rest of the group: she imagined I was secretly a gifted detective. Of course I protested vigorously, but somehow the more I protested, the more firmly they believed this ridiculous idea. "It's so strange," she said, "to be suddenly transported from everyday life, into the middle of a mystery novel. Ordinarily, I don't read mystery novels. Most of them are really trash; they're so badly written, and totally preposterous. Of course, not all of them—do you like P. D. James? I find her fascinating."

Unfortunately, I was as deficient with regard to P. D. James as I was with regard to Emily Dickinson. I avoided talking about my reading habits. "Frankly, Victoria," I said, "about this awful matter, you know, Gerald's death.... I haven't got a clue. You're as likely to figure it out as I am. After all, you were there that night. Incidentally, I'm eternally grateful that Celia wasn't at the meeting. It must be just plain traumatic, the whole thing. Personally, I'm trying to stay out of the whole affair."

"Oh, Frank. Don't be so modest. Do you know what book we read last month? Before the chickpea novel."

"Celia tells me the names of the books, but I never remember them."

"It was a mystery novel actually—but a quite literary one. It was called *Ricochet*. It was something vaguely like a movie you might know, *Strangers on a Train*, if you saw that one; Alfred Hitchcock directed it."

"I did see it. Years ago. Barely remember it. Something to do with tennis?"

"There's a scene at a tennis match; but that's not the point. The movie, and this book, they had a common theme. Two people exchange murders. They make an arrangement. One of them says, I'll kill the person you want dead, you'll kill the person I want dead; that way, nobody will suspect either of us. Because neither of us will have a motive. You get the point? The book used that device. The main character, a woman named Zelda, wants her husband dead; at a cocktail party, she meets another woman, Madeleine, who also wants her husband dead. And they decide to exchange murders. Madeleine's husband is an artist, Gregory, and Zelda falls in love with him... but meanwhile, Madeleine kills Zelda's husband, Roger.... Anyway, the whole thing is very intense, and it explores themes about love and hate and revenge, and the writing is extremely beautiful, in a baroque sort of way...."

"OK, Victoria, but what are you driving at?"

"That's my theory here. Remember, we all read this book. And maybe it planted an idea in peoples' minds. What I'm saying is, I think one of the women killed Gerald. I'm not saying they had anything against Gerald, but if they thought, well, nobody would ever know, because they wouldn't have a motive...."

"But why kill him during the meeting of the book club? Doesn't that seem peculiar? And wouldn't that mean, if this ricochet thing is right, that there's somebody else, somebody who would be expected to kill somebody else?"

"Frank, I admit, it's a horrible thought. But there's something poetic about it... something almost grand. Imagine,

Frank, *two* murderesses, in one little book club, and think of the plotting and... how *dark* it is, how literary.... So the question is: who could it be. Well, I rule myself out; I know I didn't kill anybody. And Henrietta, of course.... She's much too old. But, on the other hand, there's Grace...."

"Grace? Why do you say Grace?

"Grace is a sociopath. I really think so. We're supposed to be close friends. And we *are* close. Close enough for me to see what's wrong with her."

"You really think Grace is capable of murder?"

"Oh, definitely. Beyond a doubt."

"But... I heard—this surprises me, Victoria, I mean, coming from you. What I heard was that you and she were supposed to be, uh, well, you know involved, that is, with each other...."

"Oh, Frank, you're so antediluvian. Why don't you just say what you mean? That we were lovers? Yes, we were. For a while. But really, Frank, it didn't last, it was impossible, she's a control freak, and her sexual appetites—well, never mind. Anyway, I think she wants to get rid of one of her ex-husbands. Of course, they're divorced and all that, but she hates him, and if he died she'd get some of his money, that's part of the divorce arrangement. She loves money. And I think she'd love the idea of killing somebody. It would titillate her. Almost sexually. Believe me, Frank, I know that woman. She's capable of absolutely *anything*."

"So, let me get this straight. You think she killed Gerald, and now expects somebody else to kill her ex-husband?"

"Exactly."

I thought this was complete nonsense, but I kept my thoughts to myself. "And... this second murderer, that would be who?"

"That's obvious, Frank. Millie, of course. She's the one who wanted to get rid of Gerald, no? So now Millie has to do the other half, that is, Grace's ex-husband."

"You know, Victoria," I said, "I'm having trouble with that theory. It's too far-fetched. And how could Grace do it? Did she have time? Are you saying she raced to the back of the house and killed Gerald? When?"

"Oh, whenever. How long does it take?"

"I have no idea. I never smothered anybody. I think you can't do it in two minutes.... Did Grace, well, disappear into the back of the house?"

"She could have. I wasn't watching."

I had to say it: "I heard that *you* were the one that left the living room, and were gone for some considerable time. Is that true, Victoria?"

She seemed startled. And frightened? I had trouble reading her expression. She paused for a second or two, and then said: "Me? Really, that's nonsense.... How long was I supposed to be gone?"

"A while. I don't really know. Somebody told me that."

"Who, Frank?"

"I'd rather not say." And, emboldened, I plunged right in: "And, they said, you were having an affair with Gerald.... Were you, Victoria?"

"Frank, why are you quizzing me? I refuse to answer such questions. Really, Frank, it's none of your business. And don't take this refusal to answer as a sort of confession, I mean, that there really was something between us. Anyway, I didn't kill him, if that's what you're after. Yes, I went to the bathroom... maybe I was there a long time. Sometimes that happens. I don't have to draw you a picture. There are, you know, certain bodily functions.... The whole idea is ridiculous."

I was getting quite uncomfortable, and I wondered why Victoria had come to see me. She didn't seem to have any *legal* business with me; she wanted merely to talk about the case, and she, like the rest of them, came out with the absurd idea that I had some gift for solving murder cases. Or was the point to launch this other absurd idea, the one about the two murders, only one of which had happened so far? Was she serious about that? Or was it part of an elaborate charade? Victoria was, after all, a suspect, whether she knew it or not. Was she trying to shift attention from herself?

She got up to go. But she paused at the door, turned, and said: "Frank... is that what people are saying? That Gerald and I were having an affair?"

"Well, I wouldn't say that 'people' are saying it, but at least one person thinks so, yes."

"And you won't tell me who. All right. But I think you should know, then, that I *am* involved with somebody. And it isn't Gerald. Somebody really wonderful—and I'm very much in love. But I won't give you a name."

"I don't need to know, Victoria."

"It's something new in my life. Somebody very attractive," she said. "And, though I know this sounds odd, somebody dangerous. I mean, seriously dangerous."

"Dangerous, Victoria? In what sense?"

"I shouldn't be telling you this. I mean it quite literally: dangerous. Maybe that's the attraction. I'm drawn to this kind of danger, like a moth to the flame. You know, men are attracted to danger, aren't they? They climb mountains, join armies, and go hang-gliding—all sorts of crazy, dangerous things. Women don't do the same sorts of things; they don't climb mountains or fight wars. It's sexual danger that attracts them. The hint of something wild, something animal-like. And that's the position I'm in. I don't know why I'm telling you this. I shouldn't be. But I know you're discreet."

"Yes, I am discreet," I said.

I did feel a little embarrassed. I am, to be sure, a male. But attracted to danger? Most definitely not. I never climbed a mountain in my life (and plenty of women do). I never joined anybody's army, or the French Foreign Legion. My cousin Mitch was an avid hang-glider, and once tried to talk me into "having a go at it." Wild horses couldn't drag me into any such thing.

But I couldn't help wondering, though, who could this be, Victoria's dangerous lover? And what was dangerous about him? But I didn't get an answer—not then, anyway.

Victoria was at the door, but instead of leaving, she turned around, came back into my office, and sat herself down on the chair. She had obviously thought of something she wanted to say—or else it was something she had decided not to say, but now she changed her mind. "Frank," she said, "I need to ask you something. You're the only lawyer I really know. And trust. You can keep a secret; you're discreet, and you have a lot of common sense."

"Well, I try," I said.

"Can you answer a question? I heard people say, if you go to Brazil, a criminal, let's say, that this country can't get you back. Is that true, Frank?"

"I honestly don't know. I've heard something along those lines, yes. But it's not exactly my field. I could look it up, though. What you're saying is, you think there's no extradition treaty between us and Brazil."

"Can you find out? I'll pay you, of course. And, oh yes, if not Brazil, are there other countries? Countries where, if you run away, they can't get you back?"

"Victoria, I can't help asking: why do you want to know?"

"I can't tell you. Not now."

"Victoria, if I'm going to be your lawyer, you have to trust me entirely. You shouldn't keep secrets from me."

"Why not, Frank? I just asked you to find something out, write a memo, or tell me—that's all. A legal question. I don't have to say any more. You're my lawyer, yes; but I don't have to tell you every last detail of my personal life, isn't that so?"

I had to admit that it was.

"Do this for me," she said. "I'm a client, after all. You handled mother's real estate, remember? Well, there's still one parcel—a house at Lake Tahoe. We didn't sell it because I wanted to use it for vacations. But there's a potential buyer; and the rumor is, he's willing to offer really big money. If he does, I'm tempted to take it."

"OK. But so far, there's no actual offer, right?"

"Not yet. But if he does, will you... do what's necessary?"

I said I would.

"Do I have to sign an agreement?" she asked.

"An agreement? About the house?"

"No," she said, "I mean, with you. A formal contract, or retainer, or whatever they call it; something that says you're my lawyer, and you represent me in, well, everything."

"It's not necessary," I replied. "Just telling me is good enough."

Victoria, quite obviously, was holding something back. You didn't need to be Sherlock Holmes to see that. I doubted the Lake Tahoe story. Yes, there was a house at Lake Tahoe. I had no idea whether it was for sale or not. I think what she wanted was some formal connection with me, something iron-clad, so that I would have an absolute obligation to keep whatever she said confidential. But for what reason? What was she hiding? Why was she asking about extradition? Surely it wasn't idle curiosity. Was Victoria thinking of running away? And from what?

I thought about these questions long after Victoria had left.

11

Henrietta was the oldest member of the book club group. She was 82, I believe, or perhaps a bit older. She was the next of the women to come see me. "I have something to talk to you about," she said on the phone. "Can I make an appointment?"

I said, "of course." We fixed a time—the next afternoon, as it happened.

It was a cloudy day, with the smell of rain in the air. It never rains in summer in my part of California, but the rainy season starts in the fall. Not that it rains every day. There's a great deal of variation. It makes a difference, I think. Weather of the rainy sort, in my opinion, has a definite effect on the psyche. On mine, at any rate. The weather that day made me restless; and I had trouble getting down to work. I puttered around drafting a trust instrument, but it was a relief to see clients, actual people, so in a sense Henrietta was very welcome, although I knew she was bound to talk about "the case;" and probably little or nothing else.

I ate lunch by myself, rather quickly, grabbing a sandwich and a Diet Coke at a nearby restaurant, and tried to accomplish something in the office. At three o'clock, Henrietta appeared on the dot, as she promised she would. Henrietta was thin and bony, with pure white hair which she wore in a bun. She walked briskly, even though she used a cane which seemed to be mostly for show. She was dressed severely but well, in a black dress, with a string of pearls around her neck.

Whether they were real pearls or artificial was not something I could tell. Not that it mattered.

Henrietta had given up driving, at least for a while. Her eyesight was poor; and she wore thick glasses. "I have cataracts," she told me. "I'm going to have them taken care of. But not yet. Right now, I don't see that well. Things are pretty blurry. In my left eye. The right eye is better." Her granddaughter Tanya—I think I mentioned this—lived with her; and it was Tanya who took her to the book club and to the grocery store when she needed it, and who drove her to appointments with doctors and dentists. Tanya came in with Henrietta. She was a very beautiful young woman, with raven-black hair, which she wore loose and long; she was wearing black slacks, and a white blouse open at the neck. She had a gold earring in her left ear. She had a striking resemblance to Henrietta: she looked like a kind of younger, more lavish edition.

"Tanya, darling, I won't be that long," Henrietta said. "Come back for me... it won't be more than an hour. I'll call you on my cell phone."

Tanya dutifully left. "You know I don't drive," Henrietta said.

"Yes, I know. The cataracts."

"Oh, not only that. It's arthritis, too. I wouldn't wish it on my worst enemy. I have a license, but I don't use the car. Maybe after I have the cataracts removed.... Tanya drives me around when I need her. I take cabs, too. Old age is a misery. I don't recommend it. Never grow old, Frank."

"Do I have a choice?"

"I suppose you don't. Anyway, I hate to be dependent; I've been independent all my life. I don't like asking for favors. And Tanya works, she's busy, I try not to impose on her too much... though after all, she does owe me something."

"I'm sure she does."

"She doesn't have to pay rent. That's important these days. Rents around here, they're absolutely insane. I suppose it's not what most young women would want, living with some old crone, their arthritic grandma. But I don't interfere with her life. She comes and goes as she pleases. I don't ask her where she goes. She's free as a breeze."

I nodded my head.

Henrietta went on: "I think you know, Frank, something about the family history."

I said I had heard things, but only vaguely. "Tanya's parents are dead," Henrietta said. "I had three daughters; one of them, Benna, lives in Chicago; Suzanne lives in Boston. They're both married. Tanya's mother, Sonia, she was the youngest, and she was always trouble. When my husband died, she was only seven; maybe that was why things went so dreadfully wrong. I tell you, Frank, Sonia was a handful. She dropped out of college, and got married. Of course, she was pregnant. I think she wanted an abortion, but the man, the guy, who was supposed to be the father, he didn't want that; he wanted to marry her, the big fool, and that's what he did. I liked him a lot. His name was Nelson. He was a good man, and I'll never know how he got mixed up with Sonia."

She paused to take a breath. "She was impossible, Sonia. My own daughter, but I have to admit it. Nelson, he was a gentle soul. He used to talk to me, he said, what should I do. Sonia was drinking a lot. He adored the baby, my Tanya. You know, Nelson said to me once, I'm not even sure she's my child; but I don't care, I love her madly. Sonia wasn't much of a mother. She left the baby, she went out to bars, she drank, she took drugs, she had other men.... I was horrified. Sometimes I stayed with Tanya, but sometimes I was busy, or she never bothered calling me; Nelson took care of the child, when he could. They got divorced. Nelson went to court, he asked for custody, he said Sonia wasn't a fit mother, and... she fought it, God knows why; but she won—the mother usually does— and she told a bunch of lies about Nelson. He never gave up. Later, when Tanya was, oh, thirteen or fourteen, things were especially bad, Sonia was drunk so much of the time, and the men she was fooling around with, oh my God. Then there came this terrible tragedy. Did Celia tell you about it?"

"I'm not sure... the details...."

"I had Tanya with me, Sonia had left her, and gone off somewhere. Then she came back, she seemed high on something, who knows what drug she was taking. Nelson was supposed to come over, visitation, and when the doorbell rang, I sent Tanya out of the room, I knew there would be a scene. Sonia was in a terrible mood. They came into the kitchen... and she was hollering, oh, it was awful.... I couldn't stand it. I ran out of there into one of the bedrooms. There was a terrible argument—shouting and screaming.... I should have gone back, tried to do something, but I just felt I couldn't. To my dying day, I'll regret this. Then I heard a different kind of scream.... I rushed in... and Sonia was dead. And Nelson, he was standing in the room, holding a kitchen knife, as white as a sheet, and saying over and over again, it was an accident. Of course, we had to call the police. They arrested Nelson, but they let him go, he said it was an accident, or maybe self-defense. He hired a lawyer, and he was out on bail I think. I'm not sure. But he wasn't in jail somehow. And then he killed himself, he jumped off a bridge. He left a note. He said he just couldn't face what was coming. Do you blame him? And my poor Tanya was an orphan. So I took her in, and I raised her, all by myself."

"Nelson stabbed your daughter?"

"I would have said, no, it's impossible. But facts are facts. She was dead, my daughter. Stabbed to death. I didn't think it was in his character, but maybe there comes a point, when you're so provoked, you just crack. I never had a chance to talk to him about what happened, I never got the exact sequence of events. Well, it doesn't matter, does it? Not now. Poor Tanya.... But this isn't what I came for. Old people love to talk. I try to control myself, but sometimes I just go on and on. Anyway, this story, it does have a bearing on things."

"I'm listening, Henrietta."

"I wanted to talk to you about the book group. About Gerald. I guess I brought the other thing up, because... well, it's the second time in my long life that I've faced violent crime. That night, to be honest, I didn't really want to go. I always hated it when the group met at Millie's. Let me tell you why.

You see, Nelson was in business. Something to do with computers. And Gerald was his partner. When Nelson died, Gerald took over the business. He never paid us very much; he said the business was nearly bankrupt. I really didn't care, my husband left me some money, I didn't need anything, I was getting older.... But Gerald left a bad taste in my mouth. I don't think he played fair with us. I haven't got anything against Millie, but Gerald—I had no use for him."

"What happened to the business?"

"It did go bankrupt. As expected. So I suppose Gerald was right. Then Gerald went into a new business, something similar, I think. With a new partner. But I was bitter. You can understand that. I usually tried to avoid Gerald, because of that bad history; still, I felt friendly feelings about Millie and... I went to the book club pretty regularly; after all, it was at Millie's house only once out of every ten sessions. That night, Tanya drove me. I think it was 7:30. She went somewhere, maybe home; you can ask her. And she came back at, oh, I think it was ten o'clock. Maybe it was earlier, maybe later. I didn't pay attention. I was waiting in the house, talking to Millie. I called Tanya on my cell phone, and she said, she'd been at the shopping center, or something, and she'd be by in ten minutes. So I was one of the last to leave. Well, Millie went into the kitchen, she was doing the dishes. I had to go to the bathroom... and I heard a noise; at least I think I heard a noise. I looked out of the window from the front bedroom; and I saw an old car parked a little ways from the house. A really beat up old car. I'm not much on cars, but I think it was a Honda. I have a handyman, Ricky, he does things around the house, and he has a car just like that."

"You thought it was Ricky's car?"

"Oh, Lord no, Frank. It had nothing to do with Ricky. Just that it was the same sort of car. Anyway, I saw a young man get into the car and drive away. He was either coming from the house next door, or from the back of Millie's house, I couldn't tell. At the time, I didn't think anything of it. But now... now I'm wondering, could this be important?"

"You're sure it was a man."

"Positively. Well, dressed like a man. Wearing blue jeans, I think. You know, I really didn't pay close attention. And my eyesight, you know, the cataracts...."

"Could you identify the man, if you saw him again?"

"No. Certainly not. It was dark, and the streetlights are pretty feeble. I can't tell you much of anything about him. And, as I said, my eyes...."

"So how do you know he was young?"

She stopped to think. "Well, I think he was. He seemed to be walking like a young man walks. I guess that's not saying much. He was thin. I do remember the blue jeans. Oh, yes, and a baseball cap."

"A baseball cap?"

"Yes...."

"What team?"

"Oh, Frank, I couldn't see. And I don't know one team from another anyway. But maybe this man.... I mean, where was he coming from? I told you, I couldn't tell for sure. Maybe from Millie's house, or the one next door. I don't know. But Frank, I mean, could he be the one?"

"The one?"

"The one who killed Gerald...."

"I have no idea, really." Still, what she said did fit in with some other fragments of information. I began to think maybe there was something to this young man theory after all. Maybe some outsider, hanging around the house, killed Gerald for some unknown reason. I rather hoped so. That would let the women off the hook. But how did this person get in and out of the house? And of course there was the question of motive.

Still, the concept was appealing. And I couldn't help remembering my daughter's ridiculous story, about the "dude from Paly High," who was hiding naked in a closet, and who left the house, according to "witnesses," wearing a New York Yankees baseball cap. The story was absurd, but did it have, somehow, a grain of truth?

12

I'll skip over the next few days, and fast forward to the next time I saw Millie. She was sitting in my office. We were discussing Gerald's estate. I had by this time gotten the original will and had read it over carefully. The will was five years old, which is fairly old for wills. I guess the marriage had not turned quite so sour at that point. It left half of his estate to Millie, and half to his sisters. It appointed Millie executor. We discussed once more the duties of the executor, and then, gathering up my courage, I said: "Can I ask you something, Millie?"

"Ask me something? Like what, Frank?"

"It's a somewhat embarrassing question—but I really feel I have to ask."

"Go ahead."

"Somebody suggested you were having an affair."

She gave me a sour look. "Well, why is this any of your business, Frank?"

An excellent question. I could hardly say, because I'm just curious. I mumbled something about the estate. "What about the estate," she said. "Don't tell me that in California, a wife can't collect if she was sleeping with somebody else. We can't be that backward and Victorian."

"No, of course not. I'm sorry I asked. Just idle curiosity."

But now *her* idle curiosity came to life. "Well, what is the rumor exactly? Now that you brought it up, I think I have a right to know more about it. Who is this lover supposed to be? And who is it that's spreading these stories?"

"I can't tell you who my source is."

"Oh, Frank, you're not the *New York Times*, protecting sources. But I won't insist. I'll just ask you again: who is it I'm supposedly having this affair with?"

"Well, it's Peter Sanchez."

I expected her to be indignant—and to deny everything. Instead, she laughed, and said: "Is it so obvious? I guess it is. OK, it's true."

"Why didn't you tell me about this?"

"You didn't ask," she said. "Really, Frank, does it matter?"

"Well, no. I guess it doesn't. Except, well, somebody might think it gave you a motive."

"A motive?"

"You know, to kill Gerald. I hate myself for saying that. I don't think like that at all, Millie, believe me. But, well, that's the way people's minds work. Oh, she was having an affair, and she decided to get rid of her husband; get him out of the way."

"You know that's ridiculous."

"Completely." But even so, I didn't drop the subject. "Can you tell me, Millie, how long this has been going on?"

She said, "Frank, why on earth are you so inquisitive? Are all lawyers like that? Anyway, it's been, let's see, six months. You know they were partners, Peter and Gerald. That's how we met. Peter comes from Argentina. People from those places, Latins, they have a kind of style that, really, American men just don't have. I don't mean, the old clichés about Latin lovers, nothing so crude as that. It's just that they somehow *care*. Relationships are not just something you squeeze in between football games on TV. Peter and Gerald: it's just such a contrast. Peter can be, well, really tender. Gerald was absolute zero, believe me. I know Peter is younger than I am, but what difference does that make? People think the man is always supposed to be older and taller than the woman, but that's so nineteenth century.... Nowadays it happens all the time, I mean, women with younger men."

I nodded my head. Did I actually know women who went with younger men? I mean, *really* younger men? I couldn't think of examples.

"The first time I met Peter," she said, "he had come to the house, some sort of business meeting, with Gerald and other people. He came into the kitchen and talked to me. The rest of the men ignored me. I was flattered, frankly. For me, it was like I was struck by lightning. I was utterly charmed. I know this sounds like some lovesick adolescent. I'm not like that really. But I believe in fate, I really do. He came into the kitchen, as I said. I knew from the first moment, this was something special. He saw that himself, right away. He looked at me, I mean, it was like he was staring into my soul. I just melted all over the floor. And from then on.... Gerald of course never noticed. He never notices anything. Noticed, I mean. God.... I hate to use the past tense.... Anyway: as you know, Gerald and I were basically separated. Spiritually and physically. We were in the same house, but in different worlds. The marriage was nothing anymore. A corpse, really. And both of us knew it."

Before I could say anything, she continued: "You know, of course, that I have children from my first marriage. Gerald never liked them. The feeling was mutual. Anyway, when Gerald and I got married, they weren't with me. They were living with Eddie, my ex-husband. You met my son, Justin, at the funeral. He and Eddie never got along. Justin, when he got to be fifteen or sixteen, things were impossible, you know what adolescent boys can be like, and they had some huge sort of fight, and Justin moved in with me. Gerald was terribly resentful. Justin, poor kid, just went from one situation to another. I tried hard to make peace, but it was no use, he and Gerald just didn't click, to say the least. So Justin, when he was eighteen, he moved out. I have a nephew, used to be in the Marine Corps, just got a divorce, and he had a spare room. Justin is living there. My daughter Ashley, she's in college now, but I almost never see her. Divorces can be messy. Ashley and Eddie always got along: it was a real father-daughter thing. And she gets along with Ruth-Ann too, that's Eddie's partner. She never cared much for me. Justin does."

"Eddie had custody? How come?"

"Let's not go into that. To be honest, I had a drinking problem, and Eddie claimed I wasn't a fit mother. I never contested it. It was just as well. I don't know if I'm a good mother, I really don't. Not for grown children, anyway. Justin and I, we love each other, but there's a lot of tension. Especially when he was having all these adolescent things, I suppose it's hormones, and then there's the awful music they listen to, and the ridiculous haircuts. I don't have much tolerance; I suppose Eddie had even less. Anyway, I was having my own midlife crisis. Frank: don't judge me... you don't know what it's like, when you have a drinking problem. I gave it up completely; I don't even do wine anymore. And then there was Gerald, standing in the way of happiness. I don't know why I married him. Out of desperation, I suppose, I was so lonely after Eddie ditched me. Anyway, these last years, I've felt that life was passing me by. You'll hate me when I say this, but... I'm glad Gerald is dead. I feel liberated. I'm going to spend the weekend with Peter. It's going to be like a honeymoon. Are you shocked? Gerald isn't cold in the grave, and I'm gallivanting around with another man. But that's the way it is. I don't care what people think."

"Why didn't you get a divorce? Or why didn't Gerald?"

"Oh, but it's such an ordeal.... I've been through it once already. Once was enough. All the fussing and fretting about property and bank accounts, and who gets the furniture and so on. I dreaded it. But sooner or later, yes, we would have done it. Gerald and I. In fact, we were on the verge. We were both seeing lawyers. I think I told you that."

"In a way you're better off," I said. "That is, without the divorce. You're still his wife, and you're also his heir."

"Oh, Frank, you make it sound so cold-blooded. But yes, I suppose I was still his wife. Well, you know more than I do about the will, probate, that sort of thing. I don't think there's a huge estate. And... Peter, well, Peter gets the business."

"He does? Was there some sort of partnership agreement? Do you know?"

"Not a clue. I never really cared," she said, "and Gerald never told me."

"I'll have to look into it," I said. "I understand the business hasn't been doing particularly well."

"You're right, it hasn't." she said. "But now that Gerald's gone, I think Peter can actually make a go of it. That sounds cold-blooded again, I can't help it. Gerald was all thumbs in business, if you know what I mean. He thought he was some kind of genius, but everything he did ended up as a failure. Somehow he never put two and two together; he never realized he had no head for business. It was always somebody else's fault when things went wrong. You know the type. Anyway, Peter's different. He's really talented. I just know it. In business, you have to be, well, a bit ruthless, daring; you have to take risks. That's Peter. He takes risks. He plays for high stakes. That's what I love about Peter. Gerald never had that kind of personality."

I couldn't help wondering what kind of risks Peter Sanchez was willing to take, with his proverbial hot Latin blood. Was he capable of killing his business partner, and inheriting both the wife and the business? An intriguing thought.

"Millie, I have to ask you a question. Don't get mad. Did Peter have a key to your house?"

"Oh, heavens no. A key to my house? Whatever for?"

"In order, well, to come and go...."

"Really, Frank, sometimes I wonder about you. What kind of an idea is that? No, he didn't have a key. But I can read your filthy little mind: If you must know, I had a key to *his* place. And if you're implying something about Peter...."

"Please, Millie; don't be offended. I'm not implying anything."

"Of course you are," she said. "You're implying Peter might have come in the back door and killed Gerald. It's an impossible idea. Anyway, I think he was out of town. If you're so curious, you can check on this...."

"No, no, Millie; it's really none of my business."

"And why would he do such a thing? Honestly, Frank. I'm going to forget you ever said these things."

She seemed genuinely irate—and I can't say I blame her. I had been inexcusably heavy-handed. I guess I came close to losing a client. I spent the rest of the time we were together abasing myself, apologizing, and trying to smooth things over. Still, I wondered if I was really on to something. It would be nice to know if Peter Sanchez had been out of town the night Gerald died.

13

The good news was, I think I succeeded in winning Millie over. In any event, I didn't lose her as a client. In fact, she came back only a couple of days later. I also found out that Peter Sanchez was out of town the night Gerald died. In fact, he was still out of town. I suppose this explains why he hadn't come to Gerald's funeral. I made some phone calls to the company office, and I wormed quite a bit of information out of the receptionist, a very nice woman (as far as I could tell from her phone voice), and quite credulous. She swallowed whatever cock-and-bull story I told about why I needed this infor-mation. Peter Sanchez, she said, had been on a business trip to Richmond, Virginia; but he was due back in a day, and did I want to make an appointment? Of course I didn't. I just said I'd call back another time.

I suppose that eliminated Peter Sanchez from the list of suspects. Unless *he* had hired a hitman. Maybe they know how to do this in Argentina. Or in Richmond, Virginia.

At any rate, Millie came back, and we talked estate busi-ness. We went over Gerald's will; I explained about the proce-dures, about probate court, and other matters. I told Millie to look carefully among Gerald's papers, to search for any insur-ance policies, records of a safe deposit box, or any other doc-uments that related to assets or to the estate. She promised, and we made yet another appointment.

When she came back, I asked her if she had done what I said.

"Oh yes. Frank, it was so terribly depressing. Going through all of Gerald's papers, and he's dead. You know that we were, well, estranged; but still, I lived in the same house with the man, I saw him every day, and then, suddenly, he isn't there, it's as if he never existed. I could hardly bear it, seeing his clothes hanging in his closet, his underwear, his socks, somehow it all seemed so... tragic. The papers: well, Gerald's secretary went through the things in his office; she says there was nothing there of any significance. But at home, that was a different story. I actually found something that seems like a will."

"My God," I said. "A will? Another will? Where was it?"

She handed me a large manila envelope. "It was in a drawer, in his desk. There was this big envelope, and inside of it was a smaller one, too. Here, take a look."

Inside the big envelope was a copy of the will I had done for him, the one he had signed in my office. But Gerald had scrawled all over the copy, defacing and putting big x's on every page; and he had written on the cover sheet: "This will is cancelled," and had signed and dated this statement. The date was about two months before he died.

She handed me also a smaller envelope. "This one was also in the drawer," she said, "it was sealed, but I opened it. I want you to look at it. Tell me what it means."

Inside the envelope was a single sheet of paper. It was handwritten, and it read as follows: "This is the last will of Gerald Unger. I leave my wife the bare minimum she would be entitled to under the laws of California, but in no case more than half of my estate. In the event that we are divorced at the time of my death, I leave her $100. I leave the rest of my property and the contents of my safe deposit box at Wells Fargo, to the person named in another sealed envelope, which will be found in that safe deposit box. I forbid anybody from interfering with these arrangements. And I would like my body to be cremated." The paper was signed and dated.

"What is this?" Millie asked.

"Well, Millie, believe it or not, it's an actual will, and it seems to be OK, formally at least. Do you recognize the hand-writing?"

"It's Gerald's. At least it looks like Gerald's."

"This is what we call a holographic will. It's a handwritten will. This kind of thing is perfectly valid in California."

"There aren't any witnesses."

"You don't need witnesses, so long as the whole thing is handwritten, and the guy who wrote it signs his name. He obviously wanted to get rid of the other will. I'm afraid this is actually Gerald's will. It's later than the one I have. As far as I can tell, it's an honest-to-God legal will."

"And... it cuts me out?"

"No, it doesn't. You weren't divorced when he died. So you get whatever the law says you have a right to."

"And the rest?"

"Well, I don't know," I said. "He doesn't actually name any-body. He just says, whoever I mention in a sealed envelope. We don't have that sealed envelope. It's presumably in his safe deposit box. Anyway, I don't think you can do that sort of thing legally. I mean, you can't modify your will, or decide who gets your money, just by writing a name on a piece of paper and sticking it in an envelope. I'd have to check the law, but I'm pretty sure of that. Millie, I have to ask you: do you know who he's talking about? Do you know whose name would be on that piece of paper?"

"His girlfriend, I suppose. Lover, partner, whatever."

"And who is that?"

"I haven't got a clue."

"Not even a suspicion? A hint?"

"I swear it, Frank. I told you: I just didn't care. We were both of us... going our separate ways. It was, don't ask don't tell. He didn't know about my thing with Peter, either. At least I think he didn't. I was pretty sure he was seeing somebody, but I never asked him, and... it didn't matter anyway. You think that's weird, don't you?"

Actually, I did. But I said: "No, Millie, I wouldn't say weird. People do things their own way." I was wondering, though: could this be Victoria? I remembered the story about the two of them, having lunch, and driving off together. Bernadette was convinced they were having an affair. But I kept this idea this to myself. I said: "I have to tell you, though, that this changes the whole situation. The will, I mean. And we better get to that safe deposit box at Wells Fargo."

That was not as easy as it sounds. First of all, I filed the holographic will, in the probate court of San Mateo County. We brought in evidence to show that the will was, indeed, in Gerald's handwriting. The will was admitted to probate, and I got Millie appointed administrator. The will did not mention anybody as executor (a serious omission); but she was Gerald's widow, and there was no problem getting her named to manage the estate. And then I arranged to have the safe deposit box opened—that is, after Millie found the key. Which she did. It turned up in yet another envelope in Gerald's desk.

We trooped down to the bank with the key, armed with the document that named Millie administrator of the estate of Gerald Unger. Technically, she was what we call "administrator with the will annexed," but I'll spare you the legal jargon. All that means is that there actually was a will, but it failed to name an executor. Somebody will be appointed to manage the estate, of course, and to carry out the terms of the will.

Gerald's personal bank account, and his safe deposit box, were in a branch of Wells Fargo in Palo Alto, located in the Stanford Shopping Center, not far from such upscale stores as Neiman Marcus and Bloomingdale's. We came in the morning, just after the bank opened its doors. The manager of the bank, a heavy-set woman with bleached blonde hair, and long fingernails painted bright red, met us—and took us ceremoniously into the vault, with a bunch of keys jangling at her side, and an officious air. I wondered what we were going to find. I was particularly interested, of course, in the mysterious sealed envelope.

As we watched, the manager inserted the two keys, hers and ours, and we took the metal box out and opened it. It was a dramatic moment. But in the end, a disappointment.

There was no sealed envelope. In fact there was absolutely nothing at all inside. The box was completely empty.

I asked Millie if she had any idea what Gerald had kept in the box. She shrugged her shoulders. "I thought he had some bonds, things he inherited from his mother. I guess not. Whatever it was, it's not there now."

"I guess this woman got to it first," I said. "Maybe he gave her the key and she got everything out." But then I realized, that wasn't possible. Only Gerald could gain access to the box. And why would this woman remove a document, if it named her as the heir to the estate?

I asked to see the bank's records: who had been to the box, and when. The manager seemed reluctant; but in the end she agreed. Only Gerald, it seemed, had a right of access. And only Gerald had *had* access. He had opened the box three days before he died. One of the tellers vaguely remembered Gerald. Of course, neither this teller nor anybody else at the bank had any idea what Gerald had done, whether he took anything out, or even how long he had stayed. He had, I suppose, cleaned out the box. Including the sealed letter—if there had ever been one.

Afterwards, Millie and I had coffee in a coffee shop in Palo Alto, on University Avenue. I said, "Millie, I have to ask you again: is it true that you honestly don't know about Gerald's girlfriend, or whatever you want to call her; who she was, and so on?"

"Frank, I've told you this already. I didn't know anything, and I simply didn't care. Don't you believe me?"

"I do, I do."

"The fact is I didn't want to share things with Gerald; I was busy trying to hide my own relationship. Not that Gerald cared what I did—but my case was a little different, as you can imagine. Peter was his partner. That made it awkward. Am I shocking you? But as I told you, Gerald and I, we didn't have a marriage anymore."

I nodded my head. "We never had sex," she said. "Not recently. We slept in different bedrooms. If he had women, what difference did it make? I told Peter I was going to get a divorce. I told Gerald too. He said, oh, is there somebody else? And I said, yes, there was, but I'd rather not say who at the moment, and did it matter? And he said, no, and he laughed. He laughed at me. He said, well, to tell you the truth, I have somebody else, too; and I said, well, who is it? And he said, tit for tat, I'd rather not say either."

"And you never found out."

"No. OK, I'll admit it: I was a bit curious. But at the time, I said, suit yourself. But he couldn't resist sticking a knife in me. That was Gerald. He said, don't you want to know? Should I give you three guesses? And I said, look Gerald, I'm not going to guess, maybe I just don't care. He laughed at me again. He said, you say that, but of course you care. Women always care. Even if they don't want the man themselves, they don't want anybody else to have him. Now admit it. And I said, I'm not admitting anything. You go your way, I'll go mine."

I squirmed a little, and stared down at my coffee. I found this conversation somewhat embarrassing. Am I just too conventional? I mean, when Francie Hilgard down the street left her husband and two children, and ran off with a FedEx driver, I was absolutely astonished. This was a woman who won prizes for her dahlias. People are full of surprises. Are Celia and I simply dull?

Anyway, Millie went on: "He said, 'what if I told you, it was one of your friends—hey, suppose it was somebody in your stupid book club, you know, you have your stupid meetings, and you talk about your stupid books, and she's there, she's in your house, talking about the book, and you're listening to her, and I'm laughing at you behind your back. You're chattering away, with all the rubbish and the crap about literature and all that, and you have no idea it's my girlfriend you're talking to, a woman I'm sleeping with. Maybe. I'm not saying it is, and I'm not saying it isn't.' And I thought he was being so nasty... it's not that I even believed him, but it just made me furious. I mean, I could have done the same, right? I could have said, there you are in the office, talking about your stupid office crap, and you're talking to your wife's lover, and I'm laughing behind your back."

"Of course you didn't say that."

"No, I didn't. I should have, but I didn't. But he was smirking and grinning so it just got me angry, and I said all sorts of awful things, you know how it is when you lose your temper, and we had a real argument—calling each other names, you're a bastard, I said, and he said, you bitch, really, it was so ugly. We never shared any information and never talked about the subject again. Right after that, we were both consulting lawyers... and Gerald said he was going to move out, did you know that? He was looking for a place of his own, he said—something small, something he could afford. But... well, then he died."

"Maybe you'll never know who it was," I said.

"Maybe. After all, he's dead; she's not about to make a confession, I suppose. But, Frank, is this awful of me? I *did* want to know. In a way I kept saying I didn't care, because we were going to get divorced and all that; and that was true, I had no feelings for Gerald, but still, I was consumed with curiosity. The fact is, he got to me, with that story about the book group. I just had to find out. I poked around his papers. I looked in his desk drawer, I looked in his wastebasket when he was out of the house. I found nothing really. Oh yes, part of a note, I think it was from her, but it was torn into little pieces. I couldn't really read it, but I just knew it was from her. It was a woman's handwriting, I'm sure of that."

"Did you recognize the handwriting?"

"No. I kept some of the pieces of paper. But then I said to myself, this is ridiculous; and I threw them away."

"So you still have no idea."

"Honestly, no. Maybe he was just teasing me anyway. I mean, about the book club. But maybe not."

"Would you recognize the handwriting, the women in the book club?"

"No, I wouldn't. And, Frank, I can hardly go around asking for samples, now, can I?"

"I guess you can't." We talked some more, though strictly about estate matters; the holograph, of course, had complicated things. I was doing my professional duty—but, like Millie, I had to admit, curiosity was eating away at me. I just couldn't help it.

Nor could I keep from wondering not only who this mysterious lover might be, but whether she had some role in the murder itself. I knew all the women in the book group. It couldn't be Henrietta. Gerald simply wouldn't be having an affair with a woman in her 80's—the idea was too ridiculous. I ruled out Grace. That would be too obvious. Phyllis? Sylvia? Bernadette? No, these were also inconceivable. It must be Victoria. Bernadette strongly suggested it was Victoria. So she was the most likely.

But, I couldn't be sure Victoria really was the Mystery Woman. Her identity was still a deep dark secret. And was that secret related to the even bigger secret: who killed Gerald Unger? I wondered if we'd ever know.

14

The days went by and nothing much seemed to happen in the case. No newspaper accounts, no reports of arrests, nothing at all to suggest the police were hot on the trail. I did see Millie from time to time; she was my client, after all, and we had the estate to take care of. During our sessions, we mostly talked business.

At one of our sessions, as we talked about some of the grubby details of the estate, I did feel an irresistible urge to bring up once again Gerald's rather odd way of dying. I asked Millie, point blank, if she had any idea at all, about who did it, now that some time had gone by.

"No, Frank, none at all."

I asked, was there anything she could think of, that might shed light on the question?

"Not really.... Frank, I've racked my brains. I've gone over everything that happened that night. It all seemed so *normal*. Gerald came in, and went into the back of the house; there was just nothing unusual about the way he behaved. And... the police went over everything, too; they searched and searched, nothing was disturbed, nothing stolen. Oh, one small thing. A bit weird. You know, there are two bedrooms in the back of the house. Gerald's body was found in the guest bedroom. I have no idea why he was there. The other bedroom was where he usually slept. There's a third bedroom, more toward the front of the house. Since... since Gerald and I became, well, estranged, I've been sleeping in the front bedroom. Anyway, you know, I'm proud of my garden, I love gardening. I had roses, other things, and also, a beautiful jade plant, a potted plant, I really loved it, and it was right outside Gerald's bedroom. You know what a jade plant is, don't you, Frank?"

"I do. We've got some too. Dark green-type leaves, sort of thick and leathery; but nice."

"Exactly. Anyway, my jade plant is gone. Did somebody steal it? Why would they do that? I can't imagine somebody carrying it off, just like that. Of course, I can't be sure it was that night.... I can't really remember when I last saw it. Maybe it was some other time. I just don't know."

Was the jade plant significant? I couldn't see how; and I more or less filed it away in the back of my brain. Meanwhile, we went ahead with estate business: cleaning up small matters, like unpaid bills and so on.

I told Celia about the strange clause in the will, the business with the sealed envelope. Celia found this intriguing—and was also intrigued by the fact that the safe deposit box was empty.

"It's just as well," I said. "Even if the envelope had been there and named somebody, that probably wouldn't work. I looked this up. The law just won't recognize it."

"Won't recognize what?"

"Well, you have to make out a will a certain way. Witnesses and all of that—or else, this holographic thing. That has to be completely handwritten. To say, well, I'm leaving my money to somebody I'm going to mention in a piece of paper someplace, inside an envelope, that just won't qualify. So even if the envelope had been there, it couldn't have any legal effect."

I also checked, of course, to see who would inherit. Gerald wanted Millie to have what the law would give her; I guess he thought she would get only part of the estate. But there were no children, and presumably Millie would have it all. Except of course that the will said, she was to get no more than half.

"Half of nothing much is nothing much," Millie said.

I hoped she was wrong about the size of the estate. I hoped Gerald would turn out to be enormously rich, with vast, secret holdings of Google, Microsoft, and God knows what else, or oil wells in Alaska and a gold mine here and there. My fee, after all, depended on the size of the estate. A small estate can be just as much of a headache as a big estate, but the big estate at least pays you for the headache.

Lawyers are unpopular. People call us bottom-feeders, parasites. It seems unfair to me. Yes, many of us make a living off human misery. But nobody curses plumbers, even though they make their living off broken toilets and backed-up sewage. There are companies that live off the misery of leaking roofs, termite infestations, power failures; doctors make a living off broken bones, cancer, lesions, boils, and pus. The world is full of people whose daily bread depends on other people's misery. Human dung beetles, in a way. But these people are useful; they try to make the misery go away. Aren't lawyers the same?

15

A home is a haven, even for parents of adolescents. It's especially a haven when they're not around. That evening, both of the girls were gone, each to the house of a different friend. Celia knew the details; I didn't, but I hardly cared. I was bone-tired. We had a quiet dinner and watched the evening news. The news was all bad, but that's always the case. The meal consisted of leftovers. I don't mind. It's amazing how many things taste better after a day in the refrigerator and 30 seconds in the microwave.

I did the dishes and then I took out the garbage. Men do dishes and garbage. Feminists may push the envelope further, but for now, dishes and garbage are about the limit for millions of men.

The garbage cans are at the side of the house. When I got there, I looked over the fence, and to my dismay, I saw Mona's mother, Emily Finbar, on the sidewalk. She was all by herself. She seemed quite confused, going about in circles, muttering something or other under her breath. I went back in and told Celia what I saw. I said I would go out and take Mrs. Finbar home. I'm not sure she recognized me when I came out again. But I smiled at her, took her by the arm, and went down the block to where she lived. I rang the bell. I assumed that somehow she had gotten out of her cage—I don't mean that literally—and that Mona would be glad I brought her back. Hadn't they noticed she was gone?

I rang and rang. Nobody answered.

I smiled some more, and took Mrs. Finbar to the back of the house. I rang the bell there too. Nobody answered. Was it possible nobody was home? I know Mona didn't like to leave her mother alone. I tried the door: it was locked. Mrs. Finbar wasn't carrying a purse, and she surely had no key. We would simply have to wait until the family came home.

Fortunately, it was a warm night. The house had a nice, neat backyard, with trees and flowers and a very comfortable bench toward the back of the lot. I sat down with Mrs. Finbar. I called Celia on my cell phone. I said: "Nobody seems to be home. I'm going to wait here until they come back."

"Why don't you bring her here?"

"Well... when they come home, they might worry. I'll just wait here, oh, fifteen minutes. If they're not back by then, I'll bring her in."

It was a bright, moonlit night, and after a while, I got restless and began walking about in the garden. A small path led back to a fence that divided Mona's house from Millie's. Something in a clump of bushes caught my eye. I have a tiny flashlight attached to my keys, and I turned it on. There, in the bushes, was a dying jade plant, uprooted, with balls of dirt still attached to the roots, and fragments of a flower pot. It could be a coincidence, I suppose; but I couldn't help thinking, was this Millie's missing jade plant? If so, how did it get into Mona's yard? And did this little fact mean anything?

Could Mona have something to do with the case? But then I remembered, she wasn't home the night Gerald died. From the location of the jade plant, I tried to figure out in my mind whether it could have been simply chucked over the fence from Millie's yard. It seemed distinctly possible. But thrown by whom? By the mysterious young man?

"Oh here you are. Thank God." It was Mona, breathless, coming out of the back door.

"I found your mother, wandering about, down the block, near our house," I said.

"Oh Frank, thank you so much."

"No problem," I said.

"I don't know what to do... it's getting to be more and more of a problem," she said. "She just wanders off. I wasn't gone more than half an hour, and nobody else was home, but I had to fill a prescription, and I thought it would be all right. She was sitting in front of the television set. I thought she would stay put. I am so, so sorry!"

"Happy to help," I said.

"At least come have a cup of coffee," she said.

I wanted to say no; but the words didn't come out. We took Mrs. Finbar back to her room, and I called Celia to tell her all was well, but I was going to have coffee with Mona, and did she want to come? She emphatically did not. "Frank, I'm just too tired. Exhausted."

So I had the coffee by myself. Mona made sure her mother was settled in, then she made the coffee. "And I've got pumpkin bread," she said. "I made some for a bake sale; it's awfully good." I had a nice thick slice of it—it really *was* good—and I listened to Mona rattle on about neighborhood affairs and local politics. She was thinking of running for the city council, she said. Something just *had* to be done about the sewer system, she said. I barely listened. I have many interests, I think, but sewer systems are not one of them. "And we need more street lights, don't you think? It's so dark on some of the streets. But nobody wants to pay for them, it's a crying shame." I nodded politely. Then, as soon as I had a chance, I slipped in a question about the jade plant. Mona said she had no idea what I was talking about. "A jade plant? In the back of the garden? I have a jade plant right here, near the door, I keep it inside. There aren't any in the garden," she said.

I must have looked disappointed. She said "What on earth is this about, Frank? Are you taking up gardening?"

I said, "No.... and it's probably nothing. It's just... something curious. Millie had a jade plant; and now it's gone...."

"Gone? Meaning what?"

"Meaning it disappeared."

"How can a plant disappear?"

"It just wasn't there," I said. "It probably doesn't mean anything, but it's just sort of weird. And then I found this jade plant in your garden, dead, you know, and pieces of the pot it was in."

"In my garden? I have no idea what you're talking about." I explained it to her. And then I said, too, that Millie thinks—she can't be sure—that it disappeared the night Gerald died.

Mona was aghast. "The night Gerald died? What are you saying, Frank?"

"Nothing, nothing. Nothing really. But... you remember, that night... your mother...."

"What about mother?"

"Well, she was wandering about. She might have seen what happened...."

"To the jade plant?"

"No, I mean in general.

"I suppose she might. We talked about this before. But mother... you know her condition, and it's getting worse and worse. She was so agitated that night. Whether it was just because she was wandering around outside, I don't know. She was crying, and she was talking and talking, oh, but it didn't make any sense. She said somebody was hitting her brother Ezra. That brother's been dead for twenty years. She was just imagining things. Or not. But we'll never know. One thing though: she had dirt all over her hands. I had to scrub them to get them clean."

I had my coffee and left. It was frustrating. I had the feeling old Mrs. Finbar was a genuine witness. To *something*. This witness might as well have been a pet dog or a box turtle, for all the good it was going to do. Had she seen the crime committed? Had she seen the mysterious young man? The jade plant? Somebody had taken her back home, that was clear. But there was obviously nothing to be gotten from her. The murderer, if that's who it was, could feel perfectly safe. The lips of this witness were sealed.

16

Gerald's death remained deeply cloaked in mystery. Of course, just about everybody I knew had some sort of theory. The book group women were incessantly calling each other—at least they were incessantly calling Celia—sharing their gossip and their theories; the phone rang and rang in the evening.

Henrietta was the source of another theory about the case. Like the rest of the women, she was firmly convinced I was some sort of super-sleuth. I came home late one night after dinner with a client, and found Henrietta sitting in the living room, having coffee with Celia.

"Tanya brought me," she said. "I told you, I don't drive at night anymore. My eyesight is bad. I have cataracts."

"They remove them with lasers now," Celia said.

"I won't let them do it. Not yet, anyway. I don't want them fiddling with my eyes," Henrietta said. "My neighbor had a cataract operation, and she was sick for months, infections, God knows what. I told the eye doctor, thanks but no thanks. If it gets bad enough, I'll let you know, I said. Anyway, I'm lucky to have Tanya; she drives me places. She has a class at De Anza College, every Wednesday night. She's learning something about computers. She dropped me off. She'll pick me up when she's done."

I didn't have long to wait before she stopped talking about cataracts and brought up another favorite subject, our local murder. "Really, Frank, who do you think killed Gerald? Was it one of us? I mean, the seven women who were there?"

"Honestly, Henrietta, I have no idea."

"Of course, it wasn't me. Nobody suspects an old lady. I almost resent that. As if I couldn't shoot a gun. Not that I ever have. And my eyesight is too poor."

"It wasn't a gun," I said.

"Well, whatever. But listen, Frank: I have a theory."

"A theory?"

"We need a motive, don't we?" she said. "Why should somebody kill Gerald? People say, it was Millie. They weren't getting along. As if that's a reason. Just get a divorce; that what they should have done. All the young people nowadays are getting divorces. No, that's no motive. Sylvia, on the other hand...."

"Sylvia?" I said. And Celia, who was knitting a sweater for a neighbor who just gave birth to twins, put down her needles for the moment.

"Motive," she said. "Motive, motive, motive. Sylvia is engaged, did you know that? She's going to marry some enormously wealthy man—he has a company, it's not Google, but it's big, it makes software or something like that. He's worth billions, they say. She has a pre-nup, in case they get divorced. He made her sign it, but don't worry, she gets lots of money. Anyway, he's from India, Delhi or someplace, Rajiv is his name, and they say he expects his wife to be a virgin. Well, he's crazy about Sylvia, and he was willing to accept the idea that she wasn't *exactly* a virgin; but she fed him a line about how she had sex a few times when she was young, and so on, but now she believes in chastity before marriage, she's sort of what you might call a born-again virgin. I heard all this from my hairdresser. Sylvia and I share a hairdresser. He's French, Henri is his name. Now there's a motive, Frank. I don't mean the hairdresser. I mean Sylvia."

I had some trouble following the logic. "I don't get it, Henrietta. So she's marrying this guy, so what?"

"You know Sylvia's my cousin, well, first cousin once removed; I shouldn't be saying things about her. But suppose Rajiv found something out—that she was having sexual relations with Gerald Unger. Well! That would be the end of it.

And I think Gerald wouldn't hesitate a minute to blow the whistle on her. And if he did that, the wedding would be definitely off. Rajiv would never marry such a woman. Never. That would cost her about a billion dollars. Now there's a motive! Maybe Sylvia killed Gerald, to keep him quiet. Or hired somebody. Comes to the same thing."

She seemed so pleased with herself. I said something non-committal.

I should be keeping a scrapbook: theories about why Gerald Unger was killed. And by whom. There was the naked teenager in the closet. There was the man lurking about outside the house (possibly the naked teenager, but now with clothes). There was Millie herself, killing out of malice or jealousy or whatever. There was the ricochet murder theory. There was Peter Sanchez, though not in person. There was the hitman, hired by any or all of the above. And now I could add another theory: Sylvia was the culprit, dealing out death to preserve her marriage to a billionaire from India. What next, I wondered.

Henrietta had a lot more to say that evening, but nothing that would interest the reader. She obsessed a bit more over her cataracts, wondering, did Celia think she was making a mistake, should she go through with it, and so on. I tuned out, to tell you the truth. Then Tanya came by to pick her grandmother up. I was struck again by how attractive she was, with her intense eyes, and her raven-dark hair, worn long and loose. She stayed long enough to have a cup of coffee; then the two of them drove off.

17

I didn't have long to wait for still another theory. It came from Sylvia herself. She arrived at my office, after calling and making an appointment. I had more or less given up any attempt to scotch the rumor—totally persistent—that I was a great detective and that I was actively engaged in trying to solve the strange case of Gerald Unger.

"How is it coming, Frank?" she asked.

I denied that it was coming or going anywhere, but it was plain she thought this was just one more example of how modest I was, or how crafty and secretive. An urban and male Jane Marple: that's who I was in her eyes. "Sylvia, if you came here expecting a progress report, I'm afraid you're doomed to disappointment."

"I understand that, Frank; I suppose you've got to keep things confidential."

"Please, Sylvia. There's nothing to keep confidential. Nothing at all."

"I know that's not true, Frank," she said. "A little birdie told me."

"Oh, God. A little birdie? I wish these little birdies wouldn't talk so much. I don't suppose you'd tell me what this birdie said."

"Actually, I will. Frank: can you possibly think *I* had something to do with Gerald's death?"

"Sylvia, it's none of my business. I don't think anything."

"Be honest with me. You think I was having an affair with Gerald, and that maybe I killed him for some ridiculous reason. Admit it."

I admitted nothing. But I couldn't help asking: "*Was* there something going on, Sylvia, between you and Gerald?"

"Yes and no."

"Yes and no? Whatever could that mean?"

"Well, if by something going on you mean a love affair, the answer is definitely no. OK, once in the past.... I won't deny that; but it's water under the bridge. It was long, long ago. But yes, we were very close friends. Gerald confided in me. We were like brother and sister. You see, he had nobody else. Certainly not Millie. Well, you know that; you know they weren't getting along. Gerald... people misunderstood him. He was really, at bottom, a very dear soul. Much too good for Millie, if you ask me. And I'm going to miss him. Maybe nobody else will. Millie is positively exultant, now that he's dead. It's disgusting. I'm actually grieving, believe me. Why on earth, then, would I want to kill him?"

"Something to do with your engagement to this man from India," I said feebly.

"You're getting this absurd story from Henrietta," she said. "Don't bother denying it. She doesn't keep her mouth shut. Haven't you noticed, when you ask people to keep a secret, they say, yes, of course; but then they tell somebody? Oh, just one person—that doesn't count. That's what they think. And that one person tells somebody else. And so on. In the end, it gets right back to me."

I felt I was on the defensive. I said: "Well, OK. I believe you, Sylvia. About you and Gerald. But this much is a fact: *somebody* was having an affair with Gerald. Millie knew that. Gerald admitted it to her. Only we don't know who this was. If you were such good friends, you can't blame people for, uh, drawing certain conclusions."

"And what might those conclusions be? People don't just suddenly kill a friend."

"Well, the idea was that you and Gerald had a very close relationship; and then it was over, and then you got engaged and if Gerald talked to your fiancé, that would make trouble—you were going to marry this billionaire from India, but the guy was very finicky about, uh, certain things."

"Certain things?"

"Well, in certain cultures... they have primitive ideas about women, you know, virginity at marriage, that sort of thing."

"Frank, that's such rubbish. Yes, I'm engaged, or whatever you want to call it. We're planning to get married. Rajiv.... I never gave him the gory details, but he knows I'm not some sort of blushing Indian virgin.... Anyway, I was married once before; I even had a miscarriage, which rules out the idea of virginity, unless you believe in immaculate conception. Anyway, these people don't know Rajiv. He's not as naïve and traditional as all that. You don't make a billion dollars in Silicon Valley if your mind is still in the dark ages, and you believe in all that Hindu mumbo-jumbo. Rajiv is thoroughly modern, believe me. And very sensual. I don't have to draw you a picture."

I could draw my own pictures.

Sylvia went on: "Henrietta... is poisonous. And worse. Don't think that she's harmless, just because she's as old as the hills. If you're looking for a suspect, you might try Henrietta herself. Imagine her gall—trying to pin the blame on me."

"Really, Sylvia...."

"Oh, Frank, please. I know she came to see you. She's the source of all these stories. I wouldn't put anything past her. But maybe you don't know the history, how we got to know Henrietta. Did you know it was through Gerald? This was years ago. Gerald had gone into some sort of business. His first partner was Nelson Crump, Henrietta's son-in-law. And Hayden Gort, that was the man I was married to at the time; and he also worked for the company. Gerald knew all about the family tragedy, the one in Henrietta's family, how her daughter got killed, and the son-in-law killed himself and all that—only he had a very different take on it. Henrietta tells her own version to everybody, to get their sympathy. She's really as cold as ice. Gerald thought she was lying through her teeth.

In fact, Gerald felt strongly that the whole story was a lie. He thinks it was Henrietta who got rid of Sonia, and poor Nelson took the blame."

"But Sylvia, why would she do that? Her own daughter?"

"She wanted the child. She wanted Tanya. She knew Sonia was no good. And Nelson, he was too much of a wimp. I know he was trying to get custody, but Henrietta was behind all that, Henrietta was pulling the strings. Gerald didn't know the exact details. But it was all Henrietta, he was convinced of that. She thought she could get control of the child. And she and her daughter weren't on speaking terms. They hated each other."

"But... but... if it was Henrietta who was actually guilty, why would Nelson jump off the bridge? Didn't people explain the suicide in terms of what he did? I mean, that he was so consumed with guilt, he just didn't want to go on living?"

"Nelson was heartbroken; that much I think was true. Maybe he wanted to take the blame, who knows? He was a depressive to begin with. You think he hadn't tried something like that before? He took pills once, they had to pump his stomach. Really. The whole thing, the tragedy, his wife's death, maybe he still loved her, and the publicity, the notoriety; I suppose it pushed him over the edge. And of course, it was a godsend for Henrietta. Now she could say, you see, he was the one who did it, he did the deed, and then he was so overcome with remorse, or so afraid of prison or whatever, that he jumped off the bridge. Then nobody would bother investigating what really happened."

"And... Gerald knew about all this?"

"I'm sure he did. Nelson was his friend. I think he heard it directly from Nelson. Maybe that very day. Gerald didn't say so, in so many words; and of course, he had no idea that Nelson was going to kill himself.... Anyway, my theory is this: Gerald knew the truth. He got it from the horse's mouth. It troubled him. Naturally. It would trouble anybody. Maybe he told Nelson, you're a damn fool to take the blame. Tell the police what you know. Then... well, with Nelson dead, it was too late, in a way. The damage was done."

"How did you come to know all this?"

"From Gerald. He told me."

"And... he never went to the police...."

"What would the point be? Mind you, he couldn't prove anything. It was just a theory. Based, I suppose, on some hints Nelson dropped. Anyway, there was also the child, Tanya. She was a teenager at the time. There was already so much tragedy in her life. And the only fixed point in her life was her grandmother.... To this day, I'm sure Tanya knows nothing about any of this. I'm sure she'd be horrified."

Something about this just didn't make sense to me. "But... if Nelson knew Henrietta was a killer, why would he want her to raise the child? Wouldn't he try to do something about it? And once he was dead, wouldn't Gerald feel he had to intervene? To rescue Tanya from Henrietta?"

"But how could he rescue her? Tanya's parents were dead. There was nobody else. The kid would go into foster care, or just go adrift. So Gerald just kept his mouth shut. Gerald... or, well, maybe he just didn't care. Why would he? Tanya was nothing to him. Neither was Henrietta."

"And you think Henrietta... after all these years...."

She said: "I do. I think Henrietta was afraid of Gerald. She thought he was going to talk. Finally. He was going to tell the whole story. And that was something she couldn't tolerate."

"But why would he talk? Now, after all this time? Years and years had gone by."

"Because... the situation changed... he had a reason. I'm not sure of this. It's just a guess. A wild guess. I don't have any proof. But I think somehow he met Tanya, and.... I think he liked her. Well, more than that."

"They were in love?"

"Frank, this is just speculation. But let's suppose it's true. Gerald meets Tanya. They start seeing each other. Tanya is very attached to her grandmother; Henrietta cannot under any circumstances allow Gerald to get involved. But Gerald has a secret weapon. He can tell Tanya the truth about her grandmother. Henrietta decides to take action...."

"You *know* this?"

"No. I don't *know* anything. I told you, it's just a guess. But it's the only thing that makes sense to me. And I do know that Gerald was thinking of going to the police. He hinted at that, when we were talking. And then... well, somebody killed him before that could happen."

"But Henrietta? How could she do it?"

"Why not?"

"She's an old lady," I said. "I can't picture her killing anybody. And did she have time?"

"Frank, I don't know all the answers," she said. "Maybe she hired somebody. I mean, how about that man, the young man, the one who was hanging around the house? Maybe he was the person she hired. Who knows?"

"But, Sylvia, that man, he just couldn't have been a hitman. I mean, if you hired somebody to murder somebody else, they would be crazy to do it when there's a house full of people; and anyway, how did he get in? And wouldn't he shoot the victim? I didn't think hitmen smothered people."

"Maybe they do," she said. "I have no idea. Are you some sort of expert on what hired killers do, and how they do it?"

I had to admit my ignorance. My knowledge of such people was derived entirely from movies. There was one movie I saw, I don't remember the name, but it was a married couple, very big stars, and they were both hired killers, but they didn't know it, I mean, he knew *he* was a hired killer, and she knew *she* was a hired killer, but they didn't know that the other one was in the same business. And then they were hired to kill each other. I can't remember the ending. I don't think they actually killed each other. Of course, it was just a movie. I'm sure hitmen don't look like Brad Pitt, and are there really any women in the murder business? It doesn't seem likely.

I had sneered at the idea that you can hire a hitman off the internet. But maybe you can. After all, you can get anything you want—a sex partner, for example, a stuffed owl, the Gutenberg Bible, antique underwear—absolutely anything, on some website, or through a social network or whatever. There was this German lunatic who killed and ate another guy. The guy was a willing victim, who answered a request on the internet. The victim was even crazier than the cannibal. He was eager to provide a tasty meal, and to star in a disgusting video, for the benefit of this Teutonic psychopath. It takes all kinds to make a world, according to the cliché. And all of those allkinds are talking to each other on the internet, explaining how to make atom bombs, how to cook and eat each other, and God knows what else.

It scares me. And it kind of makes me wonder exactly what my daughters see on their computer screens with the door closed, and who they communicate with. It makes me wonder too why we were ever so stupid as to provide them with smartphones, laptops, and the rest of the paraphernalia.

18

Anyway, if I had a scrapbook, which I don't, I could put in Sylvia's theory as the latest entry. Henrietta arranged to have Gerald killed. He had fallen in love with Tanya, and he had information that he could use against Henrietta, as a kind of emotional blackmail. I was just as skeptical about this theory as about the others, but I really wished I could find a way to test whether any of them had even a slight grain of truth.

I suppose each woman had her own suspicion. Some I guess they shared with other women; some they didn't. But what they all did know, apparently, was that they all had been talking to me. I was definitely part of the gossip. The rumor was, I was hot on the trail of... something. No amount of denials had any impact, even when backed up by Celia. On the other hand, I *was* the repository of everybody's theory. The Henrietta theory, and the Gerald–Tanya connection, was only the latest. And not fated to be the last.

Did I believe any of the theories? So far, not really. What Sylvia told me seemed as dubious as all the others. Was there any way to check out this alleged affair between Gerald and Tanya? I couldn't think of any convenient way. But then fate stepped in. Fate has a habit of doing that. One evening, when Celia was out at some sort of meeting—teacher training or whatever—I answered the phone; it was Henrietta. She wanted to speak to Celia. Normally, I would just hang up and take the message. But not this time.

"How have you been, Henrietta? All of this fuss, you know; it must be very upsetting, I suppose."

"All of what fuss, Frank?"

"The murder. Gerald. You know. You and I talked about it."

"I try not to think about it," she said. "I have other problems," she added, and naturally she mentioned her cataracts. "I think they're getting worse. The other day I said to Tanya, is it foggy outside? Everything was so blurry. She said, no, it's a bright clear day."

I passed up the chance to give medical advice. I went back to the original subject: "This business, you know, about Gerald; it must have been terribly traumatic for Tanya," I said, slyly.

"Tanya? Why on earth, Frank? They hardly knew each other."

"Oh? I thought, somehow, they were good friends."

"Tanya and Gerald? Good grief, Frank. I don't think Tanya would know him from Adam, if she met him on the street. What is this all about?"

"Nothing, nothing, Henrietta. I was just asking out of, uh, politeness."

"Politeness?" Was there an edge to her voice? Maybe I had offended her. I found some clumsy way to change the subject, and I told her I'd have Celia call her back.

Was Henrietta telling the truth? If so—and I had no reason to doubt her—then the idea that Tanya and Gerald were lovers, that was nonsense, and deserved to be put in the discard pile. Along with the rest of the theories, no doubt.

But at least *one* theory was a bit more plausible. Shortly after my talk with Henrietta, Grace called me and asked if she could come see me, in my office. "It's terribly important, Frank. I need your advice. Desperately."

When she appeared, she looked frazzled. Normally, I imagine she spent a great deal of time with makeup, hair, clothes—on strategies to overrule the ravages of time. Now, for the first time I could remember, I saw signs of benign neglect. She was overdue, obviously, for a hair dye; you could see traces of gray at the roots, something she had never tolerated before. Her dress was, as usual, too tight and too short, but it looked as if she had been sleeping in it. That was unusual too.

I motioned her to a chair: "What's up, Grace?"

"Oh... life. Life, life, life. Life's a bitch, and then you die," she said. I guess she thought that was clever and original. She sighed deeply.

"I have a confession to make," she said.

"A confession?"

"Oh, don't get excited. It's not what you think. I didn't kill Gerald. But I know who did. I've known it all along, but I said nothing, to anybody. You'll tell me what to do, Frank, I know you will."

"You know who killed Gerald?"

"That's what I said. Where should I begin? You know, Gerald was no angel. Men are never angels. I've had my share of men, I don't deny it; and I think I'm something of an expert. Mostly it's sex that drives them crazy, sometimes it's money. Or money and sex combined. But that's not my point. What I mean is, Gerald and I, well, at one time... but that's water under the bridge. I don't keep a grudge. So I was genuinely sorry that he died. But not grief-stricken, believe me."

Where was this going?

"That doesn't mean," she said, "that it was right to kill him. No, it was wrong. But I'm not necessarily condemning it.... She knew what she was doing."

"She? Who do you mean?"

"I mean Victoria."

"You're telling me Victoria killed Gerald?"

"That's what I'm telling you, exactly. She did. And I was protecting her, because we were good friends. *Very* good friends. More than friends. But... lately... to be honest, we had a terrific argument, and I was reminded what a sick woman she is, underneath, yes, she's a beautiful woman, talented... but sick. The last time I saw Victoria, we were screaming at each other, it almost got physical. Don't ask me to tell you what it was all about. It's not relevant. But I decided I won't protect her anymore. She's a menace to society. She could kill again...."

"And you *know* she killed Gerald? Did she tell you about it?"

"Of course not. But she's the one. Look, that night, I had to go to the bathroom... and I saw Victoria. She was coming out of the room where they found the body. I thought it was peculiar at the time, but I didn't see why it mattered. She had a funny look on her face. Believe me, I know Victoria. She looked like the cat that swallowed the canary. Guilty. But she just went back in the living room, as if nothing had happened. Went right on talking about that idiotic book. Only later did I realize that what I saw was so *really important*. Gerald was in that room and... that's about the time he was killed. So she was the one. There was enough time, I mean, how long does it take? She smothered him. First she hit on the head with something, who knows what, and then she smothered him. Cool as a cucumber. She's made out of ice."

"But why would she do that? Kill him, I mean?"

"A lover's quarrel. She was sleeping with Gerald. That was an odd choice for Victoria, though, I must tell you that. I would have thought Victoria would go for somebody more, well, more skillful, if you know what I mean. Gerald was nothing to write home about, in that department, the sex department—believe me, I know what I'm talking about. But that's neither here nor there. Victoria always had a strange taste in men. And women, too. Let me tell you about Victoria. She's brilliant, beautiful, she's an intellectual, she's sexy, she could have anybody; I was madly in love with her myself at one time. And yet, the men who attract her are awful people, ignorant people, I mean, she could be attracted to the likes of hoodlums and drug addicts, and even worse, I wouldn't put it past her, actual criminals. For a while, she was living with this dreadful person, he had tattoos all over his arms and his chest and God knows where else, what he did for a living, if he did anything at all, was a total mystery. I suppose he beat her, those men always do. I don't know how she ever got rid of him, but next thing we knew, she was sleeping with some sports person, basketball I think. He was seven feet tall, I can't even imagine what his equipment must have been like, and I don't mean sports equipment; besides, he had tons of other women. That lasted two months. And from there to Gerald. It defies any rational explanation. Maybe he was a relief, after that other sort of man. But there you are."

I hated to think that Victoria was actually guilty. Victoria was extraordinary: vibrant, beautiful, yes, and sympathetic. I had trouble seeing her as a murderess. Not to mention the fact that she was now my client—a cash customer, to put it crudely. But still, what was she doing in the back of the house? I couldn't be sure, but presumably there was just enough time to smother Gerald, or whatever had to be done; and then go back to the living room, for a fervent discussion of *The Chickpea Harvest*.

"I need your advice, Frank," Grace said. "You're giving everybody advice. Now it's my turn. Should I go to the police? I don't want to, I really don't. But, Frank, she's a dangerous woman. And she should pay for what she's done."

"Grace, to be honest," I said. "I'm not at all sure what to tell you. You don't really have much to go on, do you?"

Grace leaned forward and said, in a whisper. "You're right, of course. It's not much to go on. But it's a start, Frank. The rest is up to you."

"Up to me?"

"I know you're working on the case. Don't bother denying it. I realize you can't be open about what you're doing. I understand. But.... I'm not going to go to the police, not just yet. I want to give you a chance to... well, continue your work. That's why I'm telling you, before anybody else. You'll know exactly what to do."

"Grace...." I began, but I realized that she would simply ignore my protests. She would treat whatever I said as window-dressing. Secret operatives rarely admit their true identity or tip their hand. Once I had this reputation, no amount of denials had any effect on the women.

Anyway, I'm basically a coward; and I took the coward's way out. I nodded my head, as if to say: you're right Grace. Thanks for the information. I'll run with it. What I didn't say was I would most likely run in the opposite direction.

19

It was Bernadette who provided me with the next theory. At some level, I think I was enjoying all these confidences, and it was almost fun to observe the rumor mill at work. Did I secretly like my reputation as a Great Detective? Maybe. Nobody in my early life, or in college or law school, had ever thought of me that way: as crafty, adventurous, as a master sleuth, exuding the exotic odor of Sherlock Holmes, or even James Bond, although that was quite a stretch. Celia would have laughed at the master sleuth idea. That's no criticism of Celia. We love each other. But we are acutely aware of what we are. And what we are not.

So far, nobody had accused Bernadette of killing Gerald. Which was understandable. She was mousy, obscure, a woman who blends into the background. It was even hard to think of her as a living, exciting human being. Which of course she was. We all are. Living, anyway. Exciting—well, that depends.

As I think I said earlier, everybody has a story; and there's more to most people than meets the eye. That was certainly true of Bernadette—as I found out. I would have thought of her as Miss Monogamy. But now I'm not so sure. One night Celia and I went to see a movie—a rare event for us. We went to one of those multiplexes, with twelve screens, in Redwood City. It was jammed, as usual, with teenagers eager to see the latest violent drivel. I was surprised to notice Bernadette, in the distance. She didn't see me, which was just as well. She was going into one of the theaters, where a horror movie was showing. This was surprising enough in itself. The movie was,

I think, the fourth in a series of movies about a zombie from Haiti who comes to life and devotes himself, in his miserable post-death experience, to killing teenaged girls in extremely short skirts. Even more surprising was the fact that Bernadette didn't seem to be alone; and her companion, if that's who he was, turned out to be none other than my client, Schuyler Wieck. I remember she said they sometimes went to the movies together, during stretches when her husband Max, the marketing guru as I recalled, was terminally busy. Of course, maybe they just happened to be going to the same movie, and met each other by accident at the popcorn concession. But it looked suspiciously like a date.

And Bernadette, like some of the other women, just happened to drop in one evening at my home. She came to see Celia, she said. Of course. They chatted; but when Celia went into the kitchen to make coffee, Bernadette told me she'd like to speak to me, "privately."

"You don't want Celia to hear this?"

"Oh… I know that sounds terrible. I mean, she's your wife, but… this is delicate, Frank, and the fewer ears that hear it the better. And I know, you lawyers, people can speak to you confidentially."

"Well, I can see you in my office, if you'd like," I said; and we made an arrangement.

Celia soon appeared with coffee and dessert. When Bernadette left, I told Celia what had happened, and she was mightily annoyed. "That's just like her," Celia said. "She hardly ever opens her mouth at the book club; and when she does, it's embarrassing, she never gets the point. Sometimes I think it's all an act. *Nobody* could be that much of a nonentity. I wouldn't be a bit surprised if she had some kind of nasty secret. Maybe *she's* the one who killed Gerald."

"Oh, you can't be serious," I said. But I was tempted to enter Celia's words in my imaginary scrapbook of theories. One more to be considered and discarded.

Bernadette showed up at the office, exactly on time.

I couldn't resist. I said to her, "I saw you the other day, Bernadette. At the multiplex. With Schuyler."

"Oh yes," she said. She seemed embarrassed.

"I know you're friends," I said.

"Oh yes, we are. Friends."

"Were you really going to see that horror movie, though? 'The Dead Come Alive: Part 4' I think it was."

"Oh, Frank; it's not my taste. Believe me. I spent half the movie with my eyes closed. It was so gross, so violent. But Schuyler, you know, he's an expert on popular culture. And the screenplay was written by a German; Schuyler is doing an essay on his cinematographic work."

I felt it wasn't profitable to pursue the subject, which was, after all, none of my business. After some further small talk, we got right to the point. Or rather she did. "Frank," she said. "I'm coming to you because I don't know what else to do. I'm a nervous wreck. I can't sleep, I'm taking pills, I have nightmares. It's all because of this terrible business with Gerald. You can't imagine how it affects me, psychologically. Nobody knows how upset I am. You know, we all had to give our fingerprints, and naturally, these fingerprints were all over the house, the bathroom, the kitchen, but they found my fingerprints in one of the bedrooms, too, and they seem to think that's awfully suspicious. Of course it isn't at all. I was there the day before, talking to Millie, and I guess we went into that bedroom for something. But you know, they think they smell a lie. Maybe I need a lawyer. Frank, this is just *so* awful. It's like a dark cloud hanging over my head. I'm at my wit's end."

"I'm so sorry, Bernadette," I said. "But what can *I* do?"

I was braced for the usual line, how I was a great detective, everybody knows that, blah blah. She did say something about how she thought I was working on the case; but she added: "I've been thinking and thinking. I lie in bed at night, and I think about it. Max just doesn't understand. Really, I get more sympathy from Schuyler. But never mind. The terrible thing is, everybody says, it was one of us, one of the girls. You *know* how ridiculous that is. We just don't do that sort of thing. Women aren't killers. Killing, that's what men do."

I said: "True; but there are exceptions."

"Yes, but... oh, a woman might kill some horrible creature who was drunk all the time, and knocked her teeth out, and said he was going to break her neck, but believe me, that certainly wasn't Gerald. I didn't know him very well. But he wasn't a bad person. As far as I knew. Millie had issues with him, but I never knew what they were. I don't like to pry into other people's affairs. I mind my own business. Anyway, a man killed Gerald. I just know it. A young man. I've been reading about this, I went to the library, I looked at some books. Young males. They're the ones. Practically all the murders, well, it's them. Young men."

"I suppose you're right," I said. "But... in this case...."

She interrupted me. "Frank," she said, "have you met Millie's son, Justin?"

"Once. At Gerald's funeral."

"Well, there's your young man, Frank."

"Millie's son? Bernadette, are you serious? Are you accusing him of murdering his stepfather?"

"Well, *somebody* killed Gerald. And here's this angry young man, he hates Gerald, despises him.... and he used to live in the house, didn't he? So he must have had a key to the back door. He could slip in, knock Gerald out, and then smother him."

"But why... just because he hated Gerald?"

"Isn't that enough? And he loves his mother...."

"I suppose he does," I said.

"Well, there's your motive," she said.

"But this Justin," I said, "didn't he move out of his mother's house? I think she told me that there was some reason, I forget what. He actually lived with his father for a while. Then he went back to Millie's house; and then he moved in someplace else. I don't think he was that involved with his mother. Boys his age usually aren't. I can't really see him as a killer, Bernadette. Of course I don't know him."

"Naturally," she said, "his mother would say they weren't close, and he didn't care for her, and he wasn't living at home, but do you believe everything she says? She's trying to protect him. She's a mother. She's protecting her son. But don't you see, it all makes sense? He had the key... and people *saw* him, didn't they?"

"They saw somebody. Nobody's identified this person. It could have been anybody. And just seeing somebody hanging around the house, that just isn't enough to go on, is it?"

"But you have to admit, it makes sense, doesn't it?"

I said: "Yes, it makes a kind of sense; but still.... The motive just doesn't seem strong enough; and, well, to be honest, it doesn't seem very tangible, if you know what I mean. There's nothing you could really call evidence."

"I know all that," she said. "But you'll check it out, won't you? I mean, since you're investigating anyway...."

There it was again. It depressed me. The more I told them I was *not* investigating, the less they believed me. As I said, it was sort of titillating that they thought of me as the Great Detective; but on the other hand, it did exert a kind of pressure. Everybody expects me to come up with an answer. The Great Detective always solves the case. I guess some of these women read mysteries. Not for the book club, of course; the book club is much more highbrow, they get their books from the *New York Times*, from the Sunday book review section. But on the sly, I suppose some of them do read mysteries. Has there ever been a mystery where the solution *isn't* revealed at the end? Maybe there is. After all, there are thousands and thousands of these novels. There's been every conceivable type of "detective:" an old lady in a village, a Catholic priest, a Rabbi, even a cat. I suppose even actual cops or detectives. But in any event, whoever it is, the mystery always gets solved. Alas, real life doesn't work like that.

And what would they think when I failed to come up with an answer? I was living, so to speak, on borrowed time, like a financier running a Ponzi scheme. Soon or later, the balloon would burst. But, as you will see, luck was on my side.

20

Life, as they say, is one damn thing after another. You never can tell what's going to happen. The very next day, Bernadette called me at my office. "Oh, Frank," she said, "the most awful thing: there's been a terrible accident. It's Schuyler."

"My God," I said. "Is he OK? What sort of accident?"

"He's hurt; he's in the hospital; it's a miracle he's still alive. Broken bones, the poor man! They were afraid it was worse, internal injuries, but thank God, no. Can you imagine, it was a hit and run driver. Schuyler was in a crosswalk on Forest Avenue, and this car, he said it came out of nowhere, and the next thing he knew, he was lying in the street, and the paramedics came, oh, it was a nightmare, Frank. I thought you ought to know."

"I'm so glad you called, Bernadette. Where is he? I mean, what hospital."

"Stanford Hospital. Do visit him. Poor soul...."

I paid my visit, dutifully, the next day, at lunch time. Schuyler did look all bruised and battered, and he told me the story in all its bloody details. "Whoever did it, it was a hit and run, the guy hit me, and then drove on, fast as he could. There was a kid, high school kid, who saw it but he didn't mark down the license plate. The car, it was a blue Prius. Of course, there's thousands of those."

Schuyler was eager to talk about medical details, and I listened politely. Bernadette appeared as I was leaving, carrying a big bouquet. Was she in love with him? She was a married woman. But there's no sense being Victorian about such things.

To me, it was simply impossible to think of the two of them having sex. But then, I couldn't imagine her having sex with Max either, and yet no doubt such things did go on. Who knows? Maybe people find it hard to think of *me* having sex.

That evening, Victoria called me on the phone. "I was talking to Bernadette," she said. "She told me about this accident, her friend, Schuyler Wieck."

"Terrible thing," I said. "Did you know him?"

"I did. A colossal bore. But that's not the point. The point is, somebody tried to kill him, don't you see?"

"I don't see," I said. "He had an accident."

"That was no accident, Frank," she said. "Remember my theory? About the two murders... about the point in that book, *Ricochet*?"

"Well, what about it?"

"This was going to be the second murder. It was a near thing. But clearly, somebody was trying to kill Schuyler Wieck."

"Victoria, I don't believe it. What makes you think so? You can't just go around saying things like that."

"I don't need evidence, Frank. My intuition tells me it's right. Check it out."

"Victoria," I said, "I'm not checking anything out. Believe me. And how would I check it out? It's easy to say that. No, I'm staying out of this thing." Was I convincing her of anything? Probably not. I sighed and hung up the phone.

21

As I said, the detective rumor had its attractions. But I felt it was getting out of hand. I begged Celia to use her influence, such as it was; the women, alas, were as little inclined to believe her as they were to believe me. After all, wasn't it something a wife was bound to say? And anyway, they had all seen movies where the hero (or heroine) is a spy, a CIA agent, a mole, a secret hitperson, or whatever; and the spouse is either blissfully unaware, or harbors some deadly something himself or herself. The movies have a lot to answer for.

So, in short, the parade of women who came to see me, to talk to me, to pick my brains, or whatever—that parade kept right on going. Phyllis, for example. I was in my office, inno-cently working on a trust document. The client was a man with two ex-wives, a clutch of children, and a big block of stock in Google. He was a man of limited skill and even more limited intelligence, but he had taken a job at Google when nobody had heard of it, and he became a multi-millionaire despite himself. Phyllis "just happened to be in the neighborhood," she said, as the man was leaving. "Do you have a few minutes?"

"Well," I said, "I'm pretty busy, Phyllis."

"I just want a word or two with you. Frank, I hear you're making progress."

"Progress in what?"

"Solving this awful case," she said. "Getting to the bottom of it. From what I hear, you're mulling over a number of theories."

"I'm not mulling anything. I'm sick of the whole bloody business."

She said: "Aren't we all? But the sooner it's over the better. And... well, I wanted to help out, if I could."

"Help out?" I said. "How's that?"

"I have important information," she said.

"Oh? And what might that be?"

"It was about 9:30 that night. I had to go to the bathroom. Or maybe it was a bit later, I don't remember. I know we were finished with the discussion, and the girls were just relaxing, eating, drinking coffee and talking. Somebody was in the front bathroom. I think it was Henrietta, but I'm not sure. So I went to the back bathroom. Do you know Millie's house? Gerald's room... well, it's not far from the bathroom. And there's another bedroom back there too. Anyway, when I was coming out of the bathroom, I saw somebody coming from that part of the house."

"You saw somebody? Who?"

"Victoria," she said.

"You said, coming from that part of the house. What did you mean by that?"

"I mean, from that room. Gerald's room. I mean, the room his, uh, body was in."

"And....?"

"And nothing. Just that. At the time, I didn't think anything of it. Oh, maybe I thought it was odd, you know, what was she doing there? But I didn't pay that much attention. Now, I think it was terribly significant."

"Significant? In what way?"

"Really, Frank," she said. "Do I have to draw you a picture? Don't be obtuse. Maybe you're just pretending. I'll repeat: what was she doing back there? It must have been just about the time when, when—you know what I mean. When Gerald was killed. To say the least, it was terribly suspicious."

"I actually knew this... thing about Victoria," I said. "You weren't the only one who noticed. But can I ask you something: why are you telling me this now, Phyllis? Why didn't you tell me before?"

She said: "I forgot."

"Phyllis, I wasn't born yesterday. You forgot? How could you forget this? Either you're lying to me...."

"Frank!"

"Or you were sort of lying before. Or at least not telling me the truth, the whole truth and nothing but the truth."

I must have sounded more severe than I intended. She started to cry. I hate it when clients cry. I handed her a tissue. She sobbed, and said: "I never said anything. To you, to the police. To anybody. I was trying to protect her."

"Protect her? You thought she killed Gerald, and yet you wanted to protect her?"

"Well, I didn't really know at the time, that there was anything wrong, I mean, that this was suspicious. Then later.... I just didn't want people to get the wrong idea. Besides, Frank, I... really like her. OK, I more than like her. I'm going to tell you things, Frank, that I wouldn't reveal to my own mother. Or anybody else. Victoria is... beautiful. A beautiful woman. Beautiful, and, well, fascinating. There's something about her. And I found myself, well, attracted to her. Can you understand that, Frank? And later, when I thought about what I saw, I said to myself, maybe she killed him, but maybe she had her reasons. People didn't like Gerald. I know, I know, that's no excuse for killing somebody. But, I just wasn't thinking straight. Now I'm telling you the truth, the whole truth, and nothing but the truth, so help me God. Honestly, Frank."

"You are? Why? What happened now? Why did you change your mind?"

"My conscience bothered me, Frank. I couldn't live with this secret. I'm not sleeping at night. I have feelings about Victoria. But killing somebody, no, that's not something I can forgive and forget. That's why I came to you. I want you to tell me what to do."

"But it's clear what you have to do, isn't it, Phyllis?" I said. "If you're so sure of this, then you have to go to the police. You have to tell them your story. Then they'll investigate. That's their job."

"You said you knew this already. About Victoria."

"I did. Another one of the women saw her. Don't ask me who. I didn't think too much of it at the time, but now... your story, it's a kind of corroboration. Now I think there's something maybe here, something the police should know."

"Oh, Frank," she said. "That's what I thought you'd say. I know you're right. But it's hard for me. Very hard."

"Well, maybe you have to," I said. "We all have to do things we don't like."

"And if I don't? Would *you* do it?"

"Are you asking me?"

"Well, sort of... as my lawyer, Frank. You could go to them, and then... I wouldn't have to be involved."

"No way, Phyllis," I said. "Absolutely not. It's entirely up to you. You're the one who saw her. It's not my job and it's not something I'm willing to do."

"Frank..."she said. "I know you're trying to get to the bottom of this...."

This was too much. "I'm not trying to get to the bottom of anything. Top, bottom, middle. I've been saying this until I'm blue in the face. I wasn't there. Celia wasn't there. There's a police force in town, there's detectives, labs, who knows what. Just count me out."

I was wasting my breath. "I know you have to say that. I understand. And I know now that I'm not telling you anything new. You knew it already! So what the women are saying is right, you're on top of this, you're on the verge of a breakthrough."

"The women? Which ones? Phyllis, to be honest, the only thing I'm on the verge of is going crazy, if people don't stop saying these things. I'll say it again. If you feel the way you do, then it's *your* responsibility. You have to go to the police. You, not me, not anybody else. And if you don't want to, well, that's that."

She was quiet for a moment. Then she said: "Frank, let me wait, a week, maybe a bit longer. If you haven't solved the case by then, I'll reconsider... we'll talk again... is that a deal?"

What could I say? Fighting these invisible rumors was completely hopeless. Even Celia couldn't talk sense into those women. I wearily agreed with Phyllis. I gave her the week she wanted. What else could I do?

22

But of course, even though Phyllis's attitude was maddening, what she told me reinforced an idea that had been incubating in my mind. After all, *somebody* killed Gerald. None of the seven women seemed a likely candidate. Yet, if one had to choose one of them, why not choose Victoria? There was the mysterious trip to the back of the house. And then there was Phyllis. Was her story straight? It was odd she had kept her information to herself for so long. Was it really because she wanted to protect Victoria? And if so, why?

I had another thought. A nasty one. Maybe she was blackmailing Victoria. Or had been. And now, Victoria was refusing to pay, and she turned on her.

But all this still struck me as incredible. I couldn't help thinking of the times the book group met at my house. As I said, I was usually not around. Husbands were not wanted. Book club night was a rare opportunity for me; I could slip out and see a movie that I wanted to see, without worrying about whether Celia would have wanted to go along. Horror movies, for example: Celia put her foot down about those. Not that I was a fan of horror movies. The new ones are too gross for words, like the zombie movie Bernadette had gone to see. Movies about deformed, awful people killing teenagers, or weird creatures crawling up out of who knows what. I know a lot of parents sometimes feel like throttling their teenagers. But still, the teenage carnage in these movies is beyond everything.

I do like science fiction, though. Not the ones about the end of the world. I like the ones about gentle, loving aliens.

My taste in movies is not the point, of course. Sometimes, instead of a movie, or when there was nothing playing, I would say hello and make small talk, and then escape to the back of the house. The point is, I *knew* the book group. Or thought I knew them. They seemed to me, from my pretty dim vantage point, just a collection of middle-class women. Intelligent women, too, for the most part. Women who want to read books, which already makes them a discrete and insular minority. Maybe not Grace; but the others. And now I was supposed to believe all sorts of things about them: love affairs involving various sexual combinations, blackmail, naked skeletons in the closet, mysterious strangers, sordid lifestories, and, most seriously of all, cold-blooded murder. Or maybe hot-blooded murder. It simply didn't compute.

The rumor mill was intensely acute in our little circle. But it was obviously feverishly busy in the whole neighborhood, maybe the whole town. The very next day, Millie called me. She was extremely agitated, to put it mildly. "Frank," she said, "I'm going out of my mind. The things people are saying. That I killed Gerald... but that's not the worst of it."

"Oh, Millie, I'm so sorry. People can be so cruel."

"You haven't heard the really terrible part. One of my friends told me about an awful rumor, something she heard at her hairdresser's. She goes to the same place I do, that's what so terrible. I'm absolutely mortified. Something about a teenager, supposed to be my lover—and he was in the house, stark naked, and Gerald found him in the kitchen, can you imagine, and this boy stabbed him to death. Can you imagine? There's another one, about a young man, outside the house, he was also supposed to be my boyfriend; everybody seems to believe this story too. Apparently some people say *he* was naked, can you believe it, and that somebody saw him with a knife in his hand, or a gun, who knows."

"How awful, Millie." I felt honest empathy. Gossip is a lethal, invisible force, like a poison gas in the air; and there's no way to protect yourself against it. You can't fight back. There's no obvious, palpable source.

She said: "People are whispering: I can almost feel it. Total strangers, but also people I know. When I walk down the street, or go into the grocery, or go to the dentist.... Frank, I had to see the dentist today, Dr. Lindenbaum, in San Carlos—I need a root canal, on top of everything. I can just picture all of the women in the office, the dental technicians and all, just snickering and gossiping behind my back, especially Margie, she's the woman at the reception desk, the one with dyed orange hair, I've always disliked her...."

What could I say? I expressed my sympathy. "Millie dear, you just have to ignore it. There's nothing else you can do. Roll with the punches. I know it's hard."

"Strangers," she said, "they'll believe anything. But people I know—that's what tops it off, people in my own group. They think—oh, I can hardly bring myself even to say it—they think it was Justin. My son. My son Justin."

"The naked guy?"

"No, of course not, Frank. At least I hope not. But the people in my group, they think he was the man outside the house. They think it wasn't a lover at all; it was Justin. And they think he killed Gerald."

I tried to show solidarity, in my tone of voice at least. "I know it's tough, Millie. But, as I said, I don't think you can do anything about it; you just have to ignore the stories, and make it clear to everybody you actually talk to, that the stories are completely ridiculous. And they are, aren't they? Ridiculous, I mean."

There was a pregnant pause. I repeated: "What I'm saying, Millie, is that it's ridiculous to think that Justin killed your husband."

Another pause. And then she said: "Yes. It's ridiculous. But there's something we have to tell you."

"We?"

"Actually something Justin has to tell you. When can you come over? I want you to talk to him."

I was astonished. What could Justin possibly say to me?. My curiosity, of course, was inflamed. Was Justin about to tell me he was hiding naked in a closet? No, that was absurd. But then... what? Anyway, I said: "Sure. Happy to do it. But it has to be after 6:00. I'm busy until then."

She agreed.

I could hardly wait.

23

As it happened, that was a day in which I had a lot to do. My work can be, at times, extremely interesting. I love the fact that I can poke my nose into other peoples' lives, quite legitimately—though sometimes my questions go a bit beyond what is, strictly speaking, relevant to legal issues. On the other hand, drawing up documents can be killingly boring. And on that particular day I was engrossed in precisely that, not to mention doing research on the estate and gift tax—more specifically, on rules and regulations of the Internal Revenue Code, or Infernal Revenue Code, as some people call it. The Code was put together, not by the devil, but by whole battalions of devils. I'm not a tea party type, a person who thinks taxes are evil in themselves. No, we have to have them. But the Code itself is a nightmare. It is so complex, so unreadable, so involuted; so frustrating. I swear, it makes *Finnegan's Wake* look like *Goodnight Moon*.

But the Infernal Code is not your concern. I did what I had to do, wrapped up my work for the day, and then drove over to Millie's house. Or rather, I drove home and walked the block or so down my street. Our street was, as always, encased in that deadly suburban quiet. There was nobody to be seen; no life on the sidewalk or on the street itself. Every last resident was either at home or driving somewhere in their cars. The feet of most people on my block would positively atrophy if not for the treadmills and the exercycles, stashed in most of the garages, if not in rec rooms.

Actually, I don't mind the quiet and the boredom. San Francisco is the place for swingers, young guys who work for computer companies and who go out at night, hoping to "score"; it's the habitat of unmarried graphic artists and venture capital people, of both sexes, who hang out in fashionable bars, and so on, looking for soul mates, at least for one feverish night. The likes of me belong in the suburbs. And yet... quiet as it was, suburban as it was, ordinary as it was, the street tonight seemed haunted, even sinister. Definitely with regard to Millie's house—a plain, no-nonsense tract house, three bedrooms, two baths, a neat backyard. Psychologically, anyway, it had a creepy aura. It looked utterly banal on the outside; or would look banal if you didn't know what had happened there. For me, it was impossible to ignore the current meaning of the house. It was as if a huge sign, in bold, red, glaring letters, was plastered to the house: A Man Was Murdered Here.

I rang the bell, and when Millie answered, I said hello and stepped inside. I had been in her house a number of times, for this or that reason. Now of course I looked at it with very different eyes. I noticed the living room off to the right, and the corridor leading back into the house, and I could almost see in my mind's eye Gerald coming home, waving to the women in the living room, and walking back to his death. I wish I could have walked back there myself, to see the rooms where these things happened. But of course that would have been inappropriate behavior. Lawyers avoid inappropriate behavior. It's very bad for business.

I sat down in the living room, on a comfortable sofa. Justin was already there. He was thin and somewhat chinless. There was something bony-looking about him. He was wearing a T-shirt and ragged blue jeans, dirty tennis shoes without socks, and I could see evidence of some sort of a tattoo just above his left ankle. He looked like a standard-issue adolescent or post-adolescent. I knew he was 18 years old or thereabouts, and that he had moved out some time before. I had trouble picturing him as a murderer. He looked more like the type of scruffy 18 year old who dreams of forming his own rock band, as if there wasn't enough loud, screeching music in the world.

Millie asked me if I wanted coffee. I did. She said, "You've met Justin, haven't you?"

"Yes. At the funeral."

"Oh. Right." Then she added: "He has... something to tell you. About the case. I want you to listen. We want to know what to do."

She disappeared into the kitchen, presumably to make coffee. But this was clearly something of a ruse. As it happens, she stayed away long enough to cook a three-course meal. I understood. She wanted Justin to talk to me in private.

I said hello and smiled at Justin rather awkwardly. My limited experience with 18 year olds who looked like Justin led me to think they never expected social niceties and had none to give in return. At 18, I think I was different. But that was so long ago—practically B.C., as my daughters would put it.

"How're you doing, Justin?" I asked, inanely.

"OK, I guess. Can't bitch. I'm going to school. I'm at De Anza, you know, community college. I screwed up in high school, pretty bad. I couldn't get into a regular college, or, like, Berkeley. No way. But I'm trying to get my act together. I'm taking business courses."

"Oh. De Anza. That's in Sunnyvale, isn't it." He nodded. "How do you like it?"

"Not much. Never did. This is worse than high school. Bunch of dorks in the classes. Half of them don't speak English."

After an awkward pause, I decided to get right to the point. "You wanted to talk to me."

"Yeah. About this Gerald thing."

"Sure. What about it?"

He seemed to hesitate. I asked: "Was it about something that happened that night?"

He nodded. Then I asked him: "Where were you, that night? The night Gerald died. Were you here, at your mom's, or at your place?"

"Not here. Well, not exactly...."

"What do you mean, not exactly?"

"Mom said I should give you the whole story. OK?"

"Sure, Justin."

The whole story, and more, is what I got. A river of words. Justin was, to look at him, a typical post-adolescent. But not the kind that simply grunts and says nothing. Justin, once he got started, went on and on. "I don't live here, that's for starters," he said. "I moved out, the day I was 18. Me and my friends, we had a little party, birthday party, drank some beers, and they helped me pack up. It was, like, I couldn't stand it here, you know, because of that creep Gerald. Mom knew I was going. I said, Mom, OK, I love you and all that, but I'm not staying here another minute with that guy.... I'm glad he's dead, you know? A complete asshole. And Mom... OK, she's my mom, and all that, and she's smart in some ways, but when it comes to guys, she doesn't have a brain cell working. I mean it. Starting way back. And the first guy she married, well he's my dad, but frankly, he was a total loser. A mental case, believe me. Never did an honest day's work, hung around the house, said he was bipolar, that was his excuse. I mean, he admitted it, he was a mental case. You know what I think? He was a lazy bum. So she ditched him, and it's one of the few halfway smart things she ever did. But then, like, the guys she used to go with, Jesus, they were all mental cases, too, if you ask me. Or they had something else wrong with them, they were some sort of pervert. OK, not really, but I used to say, Mom, for God's sakes, why are you dating these retards? She'd say, oh, you don't really know him, and all that bull.

"Well, then she took up with Gerald.... She even married him, I said to her, why are you doing this, mom? She gave me that line, she loved him, blah blah. Later, she used to say to me, he's your stepfather, and I said, like shit he is. He's nothing to me. Just because you married him, doesn't make him any kind of father, he's a total jerk, you know? I want nothing to do with him, and she said, Justin, please, I love him. For my sake, try to be civil and all that crap; I wanted to puke. I wouldn't even go to the wedding, they wanted me to do some shit with the ring or whatever, I wouldn't do it. No way, José."

I nodded, as if to say I hear you, but I was trying to be noncommittal. He continued:

"Well, that didn't last, the business with Gerald. I knew it wouldn't. And now, she's making a fool of herself again, she's got some young Latin guy, she's gaga over him, and I'm thinking, what's his angle? I mean, let's face it, she's old enough to be his grandmother, OK, I'm exaggerating, but, shit, she's 50, and he's maybe 30, something like that. And he's doing her, it's disgusting. My own mother; I tell her, she should act her age, and she gives me this shit: I have to live my life. OK, I said, live your life, but this business, the way you're acting, it's just plain nauseating, and count me out. That was the last straw, her taking up with this Pedro or whatever his name is. I got this cousin, Kermit, he's an ex-Marine, he works for Google, he's divorced, everybody in this family gets divorced, it's like a disease with us; anyway, this guy, Kermit, I always liked him, he used to take me to football games, hell, he even babysat me when I was a kid, and I told him my troubles, I mean recently, and he said, look, I've got an apartment, and there's an extra room, you can have it, and I told mom, look, I'm sorry, but I can't hack it anymore; and I packed up and left.

"I'm telling you all this, you know, giving you background, like, OK? Because mom told me, don't leave anything out, the whole story, right? So that night, they were having this book group. It's been going on for years, bunch of stupid women, why mom tolerates them, I don't know—I mean, oh, sorry, I forgot, your wife, she's one of them, but honestly, some of those other ladies, I don't know where they get them from, anyway, it doesn't matter. I needed to get something from the house from my old room—it was my guitar, I left it there, you know, 'cause I moved out in a hurry. Anyway, I thought I'd get it; and I didn't want to barge in and have them all give me the third degree, and especially that Grace, she's a nympho, I swear, she used to come on to me all the time; and finally, I said to her, look, missus, I'm glad you like me, but I'm not buying whatever it is you're selling, I got my own girlfriend, and she wouldn't appreciate the competition. Not to mention that you're an old bag. That last part, I didn't actually say it, but it's what I was thinking."

My nod was even more noncommittal, but it seemed to encourage him to get back to the night in question.

"Anyway, I borrowed my cousin's car, it's an old Honda, and I parked outside, I thought I'd go in through the back door, must have been around 9:30 at night, pitch black outside, but there were lights on, and I thought I'd use the back door, but it was locked, well, it usually is, so I took out my keys, but shit, I didn't have the right key, I clean forgot, when I moved, I took it off from the bunch of keys, you know, I thought, I don't need this; and so there I was, in back of the house, and I didn't have the key. And I was, like, thinking what the hell, and should I knock on the front door, but I had just about decided, no way.

"Then I noticed this old lady wandering around in her nightgown, looking spacy, and I thought, Jesus, it's Mona's mom, and she's nutty as a fruitcake, we all know that—so I said, hi, it's me, Justin, you know, I'm Millie's son. She gives me this blank stare, and I notice, she's scared, her eyes are popping out of her head. So I said, come on, I'll take you home, you'll catch cold out here; but she's like shivering and sobbing, and talking stuff—didn't make any sense—and then she says, plain as day, 'She hit you, she hit you,' and I said, hey, nobody hit me... and... well, this is the really weird part... she sticks out her hands, and they've got dirt all over them, big wads of dirt, and I took her—we went to the front door of her house, and I rang the bell, nobody answered, the door was locked. But she was carrying a purse, and I looked inside. I found a key and I let her in, then I got her into the bathroom and wiped off some of the dirt, as much as I could, then I sat her down on the sofa, and I turned on the TV. Then I went back home—I thought, oh, I'll get the stuff some other time.

"My mom called me the next day, and she told me somebody whacked Gerald. She was crying, you know, I mean, she hated the guy I think, but, shit, it must have been a shock; and

I didn't tell her what I did, you know, that I was there. And the business with Mona's mother, I thought, well, who cares? But then later I did tell her the story. She said, don't you dare say a word to anybody. But now she changed her mind and she wanted me to talk to you."

"Why?"

"This stuff, it's totally freaked out my mom. And people are saying crazy stuff, like maybe I was the guy who did it to Gerald. That's like the craziest thing I ever heard. Totally nuts. Or that I was inside the house, naked, and junk like that. Look: I even heard some of this myself. My friend Jake, he takes courses with me, and he told me, everybody's talking, and there's these stories, and I went, well, Jake, just don't listen to these people, OK? I mean, it's all a bunch of bull and I'm not going to pay any attention myself; and Jake said sure thing. But mom—it's really getting to her. So she told me, I better talk to you, tell you this stuff, you'll know what to do."

Did I know what to do? Hardly. But I was glad I heard Justin's story. It answered a lot of questions. It raised new questions, too.

"Did you see anything else?" I asked.

"What do you mean?"

"I mean, when you were outside the house. Look, Justin, I believe you. But something was going on; somebody killed your, uh, I mean somebody killed Gerald. And it was right about that time, you know, when you were there."

"I told you what I saw."

"And... there was nothing else?"

He paused. "Well, one of the ladies, the book club ladies, I saw her. But she was by the front of the house, not the back. Maybe she just went out to smoke or something. I just saw her by the front door, and then she went back into the house. That's all."

"Which one of the ladies?"

"I dunno. Can't remember their names. Well, she was youngish. She wasn't that old bag, Henrietta. Dark hair."

"Was it Victoria?"

"Was that her name?"

I wished I had a photograph, but I had the feeling: it had to be Victoria. Was this important information? When Millie finally came back into the room, with a pot of coffee and some cups, and a carrot cake that looked incredibly inviting, I brought the subject up. "Did Victoria leave the house at any point?"

"I'm trying to remember. Yes. She did. But just for a few minutes, I think. Maybe she got a call on her cell phone, and took it outside. I just don't know. Why, Frank?"

"Nothing in particular. I can't see what, if anything, it might have to do with Gerald's death. And she couldn't have gone around to the back of the house that way.... Besides, your son was there; he would have seen her."

She gave me a sharp, direct look: "Frank, why are you asking these questions about Victoria, and why does it matter if she went outside for a few minutes. Are you trying to give me some kind of message?"

"A message?"

"About Victoria. Are you telling me, she's, say, your number one suspect?"

"Millie, I'll take the Fifth Amendment on that. And I'll take some of that carrot cake, too," I said, trying to be deft about changing the subject.

The carrot cake in fact was excellent. Justin took two huge slices. He looked like skin and bones; but probably, like so many people his age, he tended to eat like a horse. Or two horses. Somehow this type of person never seems to gain weight. At least not until later on. Life isn't fair. The girls his age are all torturing themselves with diets.

I left the house with plenty of food for thought, in addition to the carrot cake. If Justin was telling the truth, his story explained the kerfuffle about a mystery man outside the house. Unless there was a second mystery man, which I doubted, Justin was the mystery man; and he gave a perfectly good explanation of what he was doing there.

I tend to believe whatever I hear, which a lawyer should never do. But in this case, I saw no reason why Justin should be lying. That this kid killed Gerald struck me as preposterous.

I know that there are murderous teenagers who would slit your throat if they fancied your running shoes or the gold chain around your neck, but I couldn't honestly put Justin in this category.

Still, taking Justin at his word, what did it all mean? What, for example, did old Mrs. Finbar see? She obviously saw something. Maybe she saw Gerald's murder. I read a mystery once in which a dog was the only witness to a murder. Somehow the dog did something, I forget what, which led the shrewd detective, whoever that was, to figure out the killer's identity. Or was it a cat? Anyway, nobody yet, as far as I know, has written a book in which, instead of a cat or a dog, an old lady with dementia serves as a witness—and yet somehow tells us what happened. I suppose it's possible, but so far, no hint of this blessed turn of events.

24

Everything seemed, though, to come back to Victoria. That was something that ran through my mind. Was it possible she was the one? It seemed unlikely that any of the seven had done the dirty deed, but if I had to choose one, it would be Victoria. (Second choice: Grace). I felt I had to check something out. I called Millie, after dinner, and asked her for Justin's cell phone number. Justin, like most of his cohort, had no use for a landline; that was for old people.

"What's up?" he asked, when I called him. I tried to get him to talk some more about the woman he saw outside the house. Specifically I asked: "Was she smoking?"

"Hey, man, it was dark; I didn't see much of anything."

That didn't tell me much. But I think he would have noticed if the woman was smoking. I had no idea whether Victoria smoked. But one idea was she went outside to smoke a cigarette. Nowadays, nobody lets you smoke indoors. At least not in our neighborhood.

Victoria, of course, was my client. This troubled me. If Victoria was truly guilty, if she had shuffled Gerald out of this vale of tears, did I really want her legal business? I couldn't help thinking about this during dinner. Celia noticed that I seemed distracted. I was playing with my food—a rare event for me. Celia has an eagle eye for my psychological state. "What's on your mind, Frank?" she asked. And I was about to tell her when the phone rang. Of all people, it was Victoria.

It was a normal business call, though at a rather abnormal hour, I must say. And Victoria had some normal legal questions. But I managed to steer the conversation around to the topic I wanted to explore: "You lead a healthy life, don't you, Victoria?" I said.

"A healthy life? What are you talking about, Frank?"

"Oh, nothing. Well, for example, you watch your weight, you exercise; and of course you don't smoke."

"I never smoked," she said.

"Good for you."

"It's disgusting," she said. "I can't stand the smell."

She could have been lying to me. She might be a secret cigarette addict. Doubtful, of course. "Why are you asking me ridiculous questions, Frank?"

"Just curious," I said.

"You must have a reason."

I improvised something, about insurance rates, and her financial affairs. It was flimsy, and I don't know whether she believed a word I said, but she stopped probing me for an answer.

After I hung up the phone, we finished dinner, watched a little TV, and then went to bed. Celia had apparently forgotten her question. I had trouble getting to sleep. Victoria was on my mind. What was she doing outside the house the night Gerald died? What was she doing *inside* the house when she disappeared from the discussion? These were the questions I really wanted to ask her. But of course I didn't. Images of Victoria, Gerald, and the other women kept flashing through my mind. But I finally drifted off to sleep.

Nothing much happened the next day. I mean, of course, that things did happen, but nothing that concerned the case of Gerald Unger. It was another quiet night at home. I was watching TV and dozing off in an easy chair. The phone seemed to ring incessantly, waking me up. Celia said, each time, "I'll get it." The calls were all apparently for her.

Later on that evening, when we were getting ready for bed, I asked her what the calls were about. She said: "Oh, the ladies. They've come up with an idea. But you're not going to like this, Frank."

It sounded ominous. "What is it I'm not going to like?"

"There's a kind of consensus. They want to have another meeting."

"Another meeting?"

"You know. A meeting of the group."

"What for?" I said, trying to sound sarcastic, "so somebody else can be killed?"

"Stop it, Frank," she said. "It's not a regular meeting. That was supposed to be at Victoria's place. She was the next one up. But they all decided it would be better to have it right here."

"And there's a consensus?"

"Just about. Victoria didn't like the idea. But she was outvoted."

Victoria again. It made me pause and think. "When is this supposed to happen?" I asked.

"That's not decided yet. But here's the part you're not going to like, Frank. They insist on you being there."

"What on earth for?"

"This isn't going to be the usual kind of meeting. There's no book. We're not going to talk about anybody's novel. We're going to discuss the case, and try to come to some conclusion. That's why they want you to come."

I could see it all now. They had been reading too many mysteries, novels in which the great detective, Hercule Poirot or Miss Marple or whoever, gathers everybody together in a big room, and goes around the room pointing to this one and that one, usually making the reader think, ah, now, that's the one; but in the end the great detective identifies the real killer, and it's a humongous surprise. But if they thought I was going to do that, they were out of their minds. I told Celia: "No way."

"Frank, you can't refuse. We need to hash this thing out. We're all going a little crazy."

"It's driving me crazy too," I said. "They're all convinced I'm working on the case, which is ridiculous. You know it's ridiculous, honey. The police do that sort of thing. They have laboratories, they take fingerprints, they have ways of tracing people, tapping phones, God knows what else—they find little bits of fiber or whatever. And anyway, they have lists and files and computer programs about all sorts of people. What on earth could *I* do?"

'I know that." she said. "And I know you're right. But they're totally convinced. I can't talk them out of it. And, would it hurt you, just to be there? You could more or less monitor the discussion. Lawyers are good at that sort of thing."

"I absolutely refuse," I said. And I tried to indicate, with facial expressions, shrugs of the shoulder, and other clues, that I meant what I said. But deep down, I felt impending defeat. Celia, if she tried hard enough, always had the power to wear me down.

I hope you're not expecting this dramatic scene. Because it never happened. Yes, a date was fixed, to which I wearily agreed. But that date was two weeks off. Grace and one or two others were annoyed at the delay; they wanted immediate gratification. But it couldn't be helped. Samantha had a business trip, and she insisted that no such meeting could be held without her. Samantha—you haven't met her—was one of the women who missed the fateful session. Nonetheless, quite naturally, she took a huge interest in the affair. And since nobody could imagine she had anything to do with killing Gerald, she loved the idea of the session for its pure entertainment value. She had a wicked tongue herself, and a streak of malice, and she relished the thought of watching the other women squirm. Maybe, too, in her heart of hearts, she was sorry she had missed the big event. She had been out of town, too, for one of the biggest earthquakes of recent years. To this day, missing that event was a lifelong regret.

25

Yes, as I said, that session never took place. And why? Because of intervening events. In that period of two short weeks, a solution did emerge. And despite everything I had said to the women—all my denials, all my protestations of ignorance—I did play a part, and a crucial one, in the events that led to the end. Tragic events, as it turned out.

It all began rather innocently with a visit from Henrietta. She called, made an appointment, and came to my office. As usual, her granddaughter Tanya drove her. I said hello to them, shook their hands and motioned them to two chairs. Henrietta turned to Tanya and said—I wasn't surprised— "Tanya dear, I know this is awkward, but I have some very private things to say to Frank. Can you go and come back in half an hour?"

Tanya seemed at least slightly annoyed. I didn't blame her. "Private, grandma? Something you don't want me to hear? I'm not a child."

"I know dear. But do indulge me, will you?"

Tanya shrugged her shoulders and left.

Henrietta smiled, and as soon as the door was closed, sat herself down on the chair nearest to my desk. She looked rather excited. And self-satisfied.

I said, "Well, Henrietta... what's on your mind?"

"I've been talking to Phyllis," she said.

"Oh? What about?'

"Please, Frank. Don't play games. You know what about. She told me all about your conversation. And about Victoria."

Somehow I knew that was coming.

"What about Victoria?" I said.

"Honestly, Frank. Phyllis told me *everything*. And that's why I came. She told me she suspected it was Victoria all along. And she was right. Victoria was the one who killed Gerald. I *know* she did. And I'll tell you why."

"That's a pretty strong statement, Henrietta."

"Strong, but true, Frank. I'll tell you the whole story. That evening, and you know which evening I'm talking about...."

"Of course I do."

"Well, Tanya brought me, and later that evening, she came to pick me up. We were finished discussing the book, we had refreshments, and by now most of the women were gone. I was still there, and so was Victoria. So we were next to the last to go. Tanya came, and she parked on the street, well, across the street actually. And she came in and got me, and we went out and got in the car. I was sitting in the car, and Tanya was having trouble starting the car; it's an old car, I always used to tell a joke, I'd say, it's as old as I am, well actually, it's twelve years old, but new cars are *so* expensive, and they have all these gadgets now. Well, it doesn't matter, I don't drive any-more. You know, my cataracts. Anyway, as I said, Tanya couldn't get the car started, she said, I've flooded the motor; I have no idea what that means, but we were just sitting there, and I said, well, dear, I'm not in any hurry, because I wasn't. Tanya said, we have to wait a minute, and then we'll try again. And just then Victoria came out of the house, and she looked *funny* somehow...."

"Funny?"

"Well, she came out, and she looked around, this way and that way, as if she wanted to know if anybody was around. Of course she didn't see us, we were across the street, and the car lights weren't on, and the motor was flooded—oh, I told you that already. I watched Victoria, and she went around the side of the house, she was carrying a shopping bag, and then Tanya got the car started, the motor I mean, but I stopped her, I said, wait a minute don't go; and please turn off the lights. And of course she said, why grandma, but I said, I'll tell you later.

"And then I didn't see Victoria, she was behind the house, and Tanya said, grandma, come on, let's go. But I said, just wait. I don't know why I said that. Tanya was annoyed with me. Well, after a little while, I don't know how long, not more than a few minutes, but maybe it was longer, I mean, I wasn't keeping track. Anyway, Victoria came back, around the front of the house, with the shopping bag, and got into her car and drove away. I thought, this is odd, but I didn't mention it to anybody, and I didn't give it another thought. But now I think, maybe she had a key, key to the back door, and maybe she got into the house, and, oh, dear me, maybe that's when she killed Gerald...."

"But he was already dead, then, wasn't he?"

"Frank, how would I know? That's what they say, but do they really know? Is this some sort of scientific thing, that they can tell, maybe they use DNA, whatever that is. Really. I'm just saying, she acted so peculiarly. And... when I put this together with what Phyllis said, doesn't it point to... Victoria? I hate myself for saying this. But, Frank, don't you agree?"

Was I convinced? I had to admit, Victoria's behavior was peculiar. She knew something, or she was up to something. Two of the other women had noticed how, during the meeting, she was gone for about fifteen minutes—supposedly in the bathroom, but actually in the back of the house. And now outside. But I did think that Gerald must have been dead already, when Henrietta saw her outside the house. Still, what was she doing? And why did she circle around to the back of the house? Did she look in a window and see Gerald's body? I tried to put the chronology together in my mind. The way it looked to me, the old lady, Mona's mother Emily, must have seen something. Then Justin came and took the old lady back to her house. Presumably Victoria's visit to the back of the house came after that. Was she checking something out? If so, what? I wished I had an excuse to go to Millie's house and walk around the back, peeking in the various windows. But of course there was no way I could do that.

In any event, I had an unpleasant job in front of me. I had to talk to Victoria. She was my client. I was her lawyer. But I didn't want to be her lawyer. In fact, I wanted out. I felt I was, professionally, in an impossible situation. I had heard things that tended to incriminate her. Hearsay evidence to be sure; but it pointed strongly in her direction. I found myself in a position I didn't like. I did not want a client who might be guilty of murder, or, if not guilty of murder, guilty of guilty knowledge. Murder was not my line of work. If you want a will drawn up, if you want to set up a trust for your grandson, if you want to incorporate your pizza parlor, or buy a little cottage in the Sierras, well, I'm your man. But if you kill somebody, no thanks. Or even if you're thinking of killing somebody; or if you're an accomplice, or an aider and abetter, or whatever, count me out. Even if you did want a trust, or real estate work, or help with a small business—but you were also guilty of murder, count me out.

26

I called Victoria, and left her a message. A few hours later, she called me back. I told her I wanted to see her.

"What about?"

"I'd rather not say, over the phone. Can you come in?"

Not that day, it seems. We fixed a time for the next day, in mid-afternoon. She had a job, after all.

When she arrived, I looked at her carefully. She was dark, almost exotically so, with large luminous eyes and hair as black as pitch. She obviously dressed well at her job: she was wearing a severe but attractive dress, dark blue, with a simple gold chain around her neck. All in all, she was a striking woman. I'm sure she didn't look any different since the last time I saw her. But she *seemed* different. The difference was in me, not in her. Now, for the first time, I saw her as a possible killer. Somebody who could murder a man in cold blood. Someone who could smother Gerald Unger to death, and then (maybe) go back into the living room and discuss a novel with six other women. That Victoria might have done such a thing colored the way I looked at her. In a way, it seemed to change her very appearance.

"Victoria," I said. "This is not going to be an easy conversation."

"Oh?"

"I'm in an ethical dilemma," I said. "Well, sort of."

"Don't talk in riddles, Frank," she said, rather sharply. "Just tell me what this is all about."

"It's about, well, the Gerald business. Seven women were in the house, and it's likely, well, it's at least *possible* that one of those seven actually killed him, or, at least, had a hand in it somehow."

"I know that, Frank. You're not telling me anything new."

I was fumbling and stumbling. "So... it's been a painful period, for many of you, because of all the rumors and suspicions, and as long as there's no real solution, I'm afraid this situation is going to continue." I stopped and took a breath. Victoria was staring at me. I went on: "Some people say, well, it must have been Millie. You know, the wife. They always suspect the wife. But then some people have a different idea. And they, uh, say: well, frankly, Victoria, there are people who say it might have been you."

There! It was out. I expected shock, surprise, resentment, anger. I got nothing. The same stare, piercing but inscrutable. She said nothing for a while. Then, in a quiet voice, she said: "People? Do you care to tell me who these people are?"

"Victoria, I really can't."

"Don't you think I'm entitled to know?"

"In a way, yes. But, Victoria, really, there are reasons.... I just can't do it."

"But I'm entitled to a few answers, Frank, don't you think? *Why* are they saying this? And why are you repeating it to me?"

I had no easy answers. But she didn't wait for an answer. She answered for herself, in a cold, blunt voice: "Henrietta. You're been talking to Henrietta. She's the one. I know she's been spreading this story. And you *believed* her?"

The words came tumbling out of my mouth: "It's not... just one person, Victoria. And, look, look, I'm not the police... but, yes, it did seem to have a certain amount of logic. This is hard for me to say, really. Somebody saw you coming out of the room, uh, the room where Gerald died. You were the only one who was gone from the living room for more than a few minutes; and then there was the fact that you were in the back of the house; what were you doing there? And then, later, you acted suspiciously... you were seen outside the house by people, wandering around in the back of the house; again, what for, Victoria? Well, when we put it all together, you have to admit, it looks terribly suspicious."

"Does it now," she said, her voice dripping with sarcasm. "And why, pray tell, would I want to kill Gerald Unger?"

"I don't honestly know. Some personal reason, I guess. People said you were having an affair with him."

"Having an affair? No, Frank, you've got the tense wrong. *Had* an affair. Past tense. Yes, we had something going. But it was over, Frank. We broke it off. Totally. I moved on. My personal life right now, well, it's really none of your business. Gerald and I, that was ancient history. Well, not ancient history. But history, yes."

"OK, history for you. And for Gerald?"

"I don't know and I don't care."

"But he was angry with you, wasn't he?" I took a wild guess. "He decided not to leave you his money, right?"

For the first time she looked startled. "You know about the money?"

I knew *now*. "He had made out a sort of a will, he left his money to you, anyway, he tried to—he put it in a sealed envelope, with your name inside."

"Yes. He told me that."

"But then," I said, "when you... broke things off, he changed his mind. He went to the vault, he took the sealed letter, and he destroyed it. The safe deposit box was empty when he died. But maybe you didn't know about that."

"No, I didn't."

"So you still thought you'd get the money...."

She laughed derisively. "The money? You think I'd kill Gerald to get his money? As if he had a lot of money. Don't insult me like that, Frank. No, I didn't know what he did with the stupid letter. But it made no difference to me. We were finished, and that's all that counted. If he changed his will, that was his business. I fully expected him to do that, anyway; and I didn't care one bit. You're going to have to do a lot better, Frank, if you think you can pin some kind of motive on me."

"I'm not trying to pin anything on you, Victoria. I'm just telling you what I've heard. I'm not the police, I told you that—I'm not sitting on a jury or anything, but, to be honest, I can see why people are suspicious. And it puts me in a difficult spot. You're my client, Victoria; but I'm not happy with the situation."

"You won't represent me?"

"Represent you?"

"Suppose they arrested me," she said. "Yes, yes, I know, you keep saying, you're not a criminal lawyer, I'm tired of hearing that. I know you're not. But if I was in trouble, would you stand by me?"

"What do you mean?"

"I mean, help me get a real lawyer, a criminal lawyer, if I needed one; would you help me out, if the situation arose? Suppose I had a contract with some lawyer, a criminal lawyer, would you look the contract over? Would you—I don't know—whatever, give advice, that is, be my advocate, if that's what you call it.... Do you know what I'm saying?"

"I can't do that, Victoria. Represent you. Not if you're talking about yourself. Not if you actually did this thing. Not if you killed Gerald."

She laughed out loud. "Oh, this is rich," she said. "What, you have qualms? I never met a lawyer with qualms. How on earth do you make a living, Frank? You only take clients who are as pure as the driven snow? Mother Teresa or the Dalai Lama, or whoever, is that it?"

"I don't take people who break the law," I said. How lame that must have sounded. Somehow priggish and self-righteous. "You've been my client, Victoria, but I can't represent you anymore. Not if you did this thing."

I expected her to storm out of the office or to break down and cry—something along those lines. She did none of those things. Instead she leaned back, closed her eyes for a moment, as if she was thinking deep thoughts, then opened them.

She said: "You're convinced I killed Gerald."

"I didn't say that."

"But that's what you think. You think that, at the very least, I had something to do with it. That's why you don't want to represent me. Admit it."

"It's not exactly that...."

"Then what is it?"

I had no ready answer. She went on: "All right, Frank. I won't squeeze the words out of you. I just want to ask you a question: do you intend to repeat these suspicions to anybody else? To the police, to be specific?"

"No, Victoria, of course not. First of all, I don't have proof of anything. It's just conjecture. And, besides, I think it would be unethical. I mean, lawyers are supposed to stand by their clients. Well, if you said you were *going* to kill somebody, that's different. But I won't betray your confidence. Still, Victoria, we're not talking about something small, like fudging on an income tax return or getting picked up for speeding. We're talking about murder."

"Suppose there were reasons...."

"Reasons?"

"Whoever did this... must have had a reason. People have reasons for everything they do, unless they're stark raving mad. I understand why people are saying these things about me. I know why they want to throw suspicion on me. Don't think I don't know what's going on."

"Well, what *is* going on? If you know what's going on, why don't you tell me, Victoria?"

She said nothing. I looked at her closely. Her face was gray, troubled. I wished I knew what she was thinking. And then I had a sudden, awful thought: here was a woman who thought I was accusing her of murder. If she was capable of that kind of act, was *I* in some sort of danger? Did I know too much? In mystery stories, it's not good to know too much. As soon as the reader finds out you "know too much," somebody kills you. I had this sudden panic attack.

But then it was over. First of all, to say I knew something was a gross exaggeration. All I had were suspicions. And secondly, it's not as if what I knew was mine alone. There was Henrietta, for example, and Phyllis, and God knows how many other people gossiping about the case. Victoria was now the number one suspect. She had dethroned Millie completely. But there was nothing special about what I knew, what I heard, what I was privy to.

Well, almost nothing. I had guessed the truth about the sealed letter, and what had happened to it. But how important was that?

There was an awkward silence. I thought that we were through talking, Victoria and I. I drummed nervously on my desk. I wondered, why doesn't she go? This must be painful for her. It was getting painful for me.

And then, out of the blue, her mood seemed to change: she looked right at me, with some sort of smile, and began to talk again. "You know, Frank," she said. "One thing I do admit. I've made mistakes. Well, we all make mistakes. It was a mistake to carry on with Gerald. A big mistake. He was never my type. I have a bad habit of going with married men. Maybe what attracts me is the secrecy, the danger, the smell of something vaguely wrong and illicit. When I started seeing Gerald I kept our relationship a secret. People didn't know."

"Millie, you mean."

"Millie, sure. But not just Millie. Millie didn't know; but she also didn't care. No... other people. And then, when I broke up with Gerald... it was my idea, you know. He wanted to continue."

"I didn't know that."

"Oh, yes. Until the very end, he wanted me back. But I wasn't about to go back. I had a new relationship. Gerald knew all about it. He wanted to break it up, but of course that was quite impossible. He didn't know how impossible it was. And other people didn't know that either. They thought we were still together. That was the biggest mistake I made. You can see why, can't you?"

I couldn't. And I said so. She only smiled. Obviously she didn't believe me.

She went on: "Frank, I'm going to ask you to indulge me in something. I want you to give me one day, twenty-four hours. I'm going to try to put it all down on paper. Everything

I know. I just need a day to think. It's not just you, it's every-body, gossiping, telling each other all these things. After the one day, I'll call you or come here, I'm not sure which. I'll show you what I've written. And then, if you want to talk to the police, I'll give you permission. I'll release you from your stupid ethical obligations or whatever you call them. You can tell them anything you want. It won't matter anymore."

I had no idea how to respond. But I could hardly say no. Was she talking about some sort of a confession? "You'll come back tomorrow? Or call?"

"Yes. Same time. One thing, Frank. You don't really know me. In some ways, you underestimate me. In some ways not. You obviously think I'm capable of murder. I am. I admit it. I'm capable of anything."

"Are you... are you saying you *did* kill Gerald?"

"Oh yes. But not the way you think. Not directly, anyway. I was responsible for his death. Maybe I can make up for it. Maybe."

Then she left. I was on pins and needles for the next twen-ty-four hours. I kept waiting for the phone call. Or the mes-sage. Or the visit. But nothing happened. Victoria never came back. Nor did she call, or send any message. I felt like a damn fool.

Then I read, in the local paper on the front page, a day or so later, a startling story. According to the story, a warrant had been issued: the warrant was for a suspect in the case of the death of Gerald Unger. According to the story, the person in question was a fugitive from justice. The suspect's name was printed in the paper. Victoria was not the name that appeared.

27

The name that *was* mentioned came as a surprise—a total shock. I could hardly believe it. It stopped me dead in my tracks. I could hardly think of anything else all day long. It was hard to concentrate on work. I was so on edge that I canceled an appointment with my dentist. I just couldn't face the dentist. Plaque and xrays would have to wait.

Celia and I had a date to eat out: the girls were off with friends, and Celia decided we would eat in a restaurant. I met her after work at the Alameda Café in Menlo Park. Of course over dinner we talked about nothing else but the news. Celia was as surprised and shocked as I was. The meal was delicious, by the way. I was still jittery. My jitters had interfered with work, but not with my appetite. Especially not with dessert.

After dinner, we went home. There were six or seven messages waiting for us on the answering machine, and besides that, the phone kept ringing as one woman after another called to gossip, to chew over the news and to talk it over briskly. Victoria of course never called.

She had, in fact, left the country. Celia broke that news to me a few days later. She heard it from a friend of a friend of a friend. Hearsay; but apparently true. She told the people at work she would be gone indefinitely. Victoria had gone—some said to Australia, some said to Brazil. Nobody seemed to know for sure. Samantha even suggested Victoria was still in the country, hiding in plain sight in some hotel under an assumed name. She said: "Somebody I know was at a meeting in San Francisco, at the Westin Hotel. She saw a woman in the lobby that looked familiar; the woman was wearing dark glasses, and my friend is sure it was Victoria. With a wig, trying to disguise herself."

In fact, the woman was not Victoria. Victoria was not in San Francisco, or Australia, or Brazil. Victoria was in Paris. I know this, because a week or so later, I received a bulky letter in the mail, postmarked Paris. It was from Victoria. Inside was a long letter, painfully composed no doubt in some Left Bank hotel or internet café. The letter began with an apology. She had promised, she said, to come to me, or at least communicate; frankly, she had lied. She needed the time to have a hard, serious talk with someone, and for the two of them to decide what to do. And they had come to a fateful decision. They decided to pack, grab their passports, and leave the country. Together.

"I suppose, Frank," she wrote, "since everybody talks about your skills, you must have already figured out that nobody in our little group could've killed Gerald, none of the women, that is, simply by going into the back of the house, and getting rid of him—that would have been far too clumsy and cumbersome, and really, did any of us have time? I'm sure you figured out what happened. That she tapped on the window to get his attention, and when Gerald appeared, no doubt quite surprised, she asked him to open up the window so they could talk, which of course he did. Then she hit him on the head with the flowerpot. I'm sure it took him totally by surprise. I don't know if he was unconscious or just dazed and helpless, but anyway, she climbed in the window and finished the job. She smothered him to death. I don't think he could put up much resistance, but anyway, she's young and strong.

"Then she dragged the body into the next room. After that, she climbed back out through the window. Maybe she took a few seconds to clean up the dirt inside the house, and she disposed of the flower pot outside. Oh, she was running a real risk. Somebody could have come back into that part of the house. Somebody could have seen her outside the house—not very likely. Though as it happened, Mrs. Finbar did see her. Anyway, she loves to take risks. She's always taken risks. And so have I. Just being with her is a terrible risk. And I'm beginning to regret it. I don't think I'll be in Paris very long. I am beginning to realize what an awful mistake I've made and what a high price I'll have to pay.

"Anyway, let me get back to what happened that night. Yes, I was gone a long time, and no, I hadn't gone to the bathroom. Or rather, I did go toward the back of the house, and I heard a noise.... Did I have any notion that Gerald was in danger? In fact, I was worried, but obviously not enough. And I never thought it would happen like this, and in his own house. Anyway, I heard noises; I realized that something was going on, and when I went to the back of the house, I found Gerald dead. I looked out the window and I saw her. I was horrified, of course. But my first instinct was to protect her at all costs. She saw me, and made a sign for me to be quiet. And I did keep quiet. You see, I loved her. That's obvious. I locked the window from the inside, and I went back into the living room as if nothing had happened. Somehow I managed to get through the evening. Later, when everybody was gone, I went around the back of the house. I took the jade plant and dumped it in Mona's yard, and I took the fragments of the pot away in a shopping bag. I was afraid there was blood on it.

"And why did I leave the country, leave everything behind, and run off with this woman: a woman who had killed a man I once was involved with? I'm not sure myself. Love makes people do crazy things. I wasn't thinking straight. Neither was she. But I was desperate—I couldn't bear the thought of her in prison or on death row. I tried to bluff you, Frank; please forgive me. All that rubbish about the two murders, you know, the reciprocity murders, ricochet and so on. When poor Schuyler had his accident, I thought I would try to make you think my theory was right. I made the whole thing up, of course. I should have known I couldn't fool you.

"Believe me, Frank, this wasn't the perfect crime. The police may seem stupid, but they have labs, they have detectives, and they don't take murder lightly. I think by now they know everything. What little they didn't know, I told them in a long letter I sent. I've finally come to my senses. This can't go on. I'm going to come back to the United States. I know I probably broke the law, some law or other, but I'm willing to take the consequences. I can't live as a fugitive all my life. Oh, of course, when I tell her, there'll be a terrific scene here, but I'm willing to go through with it. It wouldn't be the first scene, and I'm used to it, to the tears, the hysteria, followed by a kind of coldness that frankly scares me. Already, I know there's some talk about extradition. I don't know the law. French law *or* American law. I suppose she'll get a lawyer, and she'll fight it. I wonder if I could ask you to do a little research on the subject. I'll spell out exactly what. I know you don't want me as a client, and I understand—but if you could do this one chore, I'd be grateful."

I never did the research. I never got any further communication. Events intervened—horrific events. Shortly after I received this letter, Victoria was murdered in her Paris hotel room. She was killed by the woman she loved so dangerously; the woman who couldn't bear to lose her. That woman was Tanya, Henrietta's wayward granddaughter. And then Tanya took her own life. She had killed Gerald, not knowing—fatally not knowing—that Victoria and Gerald were no longer involved with each other; fatally for Gerald, and now for Victoria, and for herself as well. Her jealousy, her ruthlessness, had led her to a point of no return. In Paris, things had gone badly: Victoria had come to realize, as she told me in her letter, that the relationship simply couldn't go on. Now Tanya faced yet another loss, not to mention the prospect of prison or worse. In a last spasm of violence, she ended the whole sordid mess.

Clearly, Tanya must have been somewhat unhinged. A dangerous and desperate woman. Had there been signs of this in the past? I knew very little about her life. But this kind of murderous spree does not come up out of nowhere. I began to suspect that it was Tanya who killed her mother, many years earlier—killed her with a kitchen knife. Tanya, and not Henrietta or Nelson. Probably nobody will ever know the truth about this incident. Still, knowing what we do about Tanya, it seems likely that she was the one responsible for Sonia's death. Maybe she heard screaming and hollering, and she rushed in and grabbed a knife. Maybe she went to protect her father. After the deed was done, Nelson took the blame for his daughter. Maybe that's why he did away with himself. Was it grief and horror? Or was he aware that his death would put an end to any inquiry? That the case would be closed; and that his daughter would escape suspicion? Whether Henrietta knew any or all of this, I really couldn't say. Maybe she did. And maybe she didn't. Could she be totally unaware of her granddaughter's tendency toward violence? Whatever she knew, she kept under wraps.

Of course, the news from Paris, the murder and suicide, was a sensation to all of us—to the quiet suburbanites at home. A source of shock and horror. Some people, no doubt outside of our little circle, positively enjoyed the scandal. That always happens.

Henrietta, poor woman, suffered deeply. She loved Tanya, despite everything. The tragedy really hit home. I felt so sorry for her. Bereft again, in her lonely old age.

One obvious consequence: the book club died a natural death. Too much scar tissue, as it were. Nobody had the stomach to schedule another meeting, to sit around, drinking coffee, discussing some novel, with the other survivors of the great book club murder. No, that was impossible. *The Chickpea Harvest* was the last of a long line of modern novels. There would be no more.

Whether these events had other effects on the women, I couldn't say. Perhaps there were some repercussions. Bernadette, to my great surprise, left her husband, filed for divorce, and then married Schuyler Wieck. Who knows the exact chain of causality? Gerald's death may have been some sort of catalyst.

A few weeks later, at dinner, Celia said: "Do you know Penny, at my school, the English teacher, you know, the one with the autistic daughter?"

"I do. You introduced us once."

"Well, she belongs to a book club, and she asked me if I wanted to join. They meet on Tuesdays, once a month."

"I thought you'd had enough of book clubs."

"*That* book club, anyway," she said. "This one sounds really nice. Melissa is in it, the math teacher, and some other women. It's an intelligent bunch."

"Fine with me," I said. "But on one condition."

"What's that?"

"No murders, please."

"We wouldn't dream of it," she said.

The Frank May Chronicles

An
Unnatural
Death

lawrence friedman

1

"I think somebody murdered my aunt."

That was the kind of sentence that was bound to catch a person's attention. It certainly caught mine. I looked over my desk at Barbara Homans. Was she joking? I found this hard to believe. She wasn't the sort of woman who told jokes. Anyway, I had never noticed much of a sense of humor. She was, in fact, a rather serious person. I had known Barbara for a number of years. She was a woman of a certain age—fifty, I would guess. Nice-looking, dignified. Divorced, no children. Dressed in solid good taste.

She had worked for years, some kind of administrative job, a company that made software; exactly what, I have no idea. The job paid well, but, more important, in some of the early years, right after it was founded, she picked up a bundle of stock. The company grew and grew; so that when she decided to quit the job, she was worth a fair amount of money. She had family money, too. This family money figures in this story; the software stock does not.

Anyway, Barbara was one of my clients, and she, no doubt, considered me her lawyer.

"You can't mean that," I said to her. "The kind of people we know don't murder each other."

"Frank, I meant every word."

"Somebody murdered Aunt Harriet? I mean, how can you say that? She was an old lady, Barbara. She was over 80... 83, wasn't she? She had arthritis.... Well, that doesn't kill you. But... she died a natural death; you told me that yourself."

She looked at me with a kind of impatience. "Of course I said that, Frank. What else was I going to say? It looked that

1

way. I mean, it seemed very natural. All I had to go on were suspicions."

"She died in her sleep, didn't she?"

"She died in bed, yes. She died at night, yes. But I think somebody smothered her with a pillow. Isn't that the way people do it?"

I had no idea how people do it. I never smothered anybody with a pillow. I don't know people who smother people with pillows. I've seen that sort of thing in the movies; or on TV. But I have no personal experience with smothering; I use a pillow myself, every night, like most people. But I don't think of a pillow as a murder weapon.

"It's easy, isn't it?" she said.

"What's easy?"

"Smothering somebody. With a pillow."

"Barbara, how would I know? You think I kill people with pillows? I don't kill people at all! I'll admit, I'm tempted with some of my clients. Not you, naturally. But, believe me, I never acted on these impulses. The Bar Association doesn't like it if you commit murder. And I would never murder a client; that I can tell you. I need their business."

"You're not taking me seriously," she said.

She was right about that, so I apologized. "I can see you're upset. I'm sorry if I seem callous. It's just that... Barbara, I can't believe you're actually saying these things."

"I can't believe it myself. But I had to tell *somebody*, Frank. It's been eating away at me."

I leaned back in my chair. It was a hot day, in the middle of summer. It was late afternoon, when it's often as hot as it gets in summer in California, and it was fairly stuffy in my office. The air conditioning didn't seem to be working. I made a mental note to call somebody connected with the building and enter a complaint. I was sweating, and I had an irresistible urge to loosen my collar.

Barbara seemed not to notice how hot it was in the room; or to take notice of anything else. She had a look on her face of... well, let's call it deadly earnestness. And the way she gripped her purse—it was a *serious* grip, if you know what I mean. I hated the direction this conversation was going. We had other things to talk about and this was an interruption. But I had to pursue the matter, at least for the time being, if only to mollify her. I said, "Barbara, what's the basis for all this? You said you had suspicions. Suspicions of what?"

"I know somebody wanted to kill Aunt Harriet. She practically told me so herself."

"She *told* you?"

"Well, not exactly. She said, Barbara, I have something that's preying on my mind. Those were her words. Then she, well, she didn't tell me very much. She was, I guess you'd say, somewhat cryptic. But that's what I think she meant. She meant somebody was threatening her. Frank, I think she was actually afraid."

"When did this happen, this conversation?"

"About a week before she died."

Until the point where Barbara blurted out her comment, about somebody killing her aunt, we had had a routine session. Boring even. But I should say something about where this was all taking place. The two of us were sitting in my office, in San Mateo, California. My law office. I'm a lawyer. I should tell you that before we go any further. My name is Frank May. I'll give you more of the details later. Barbara was Barbara Homans. She was my client—I think I mentioned those two facts.

Not that she normally needed a lawyer. What brought us together, right now, was Aunt Harriet's estate. Aunt Harriet was Harriet Wingate. She was in her 80's, as I said, and had recently passed on. Aunt Harriet had been more or less married (I'll explain that later), but apparently had no living descendants. At least we didn't think so. More about *that* later too.

The family situation was this: Harriet was the last survivor of her siblings. There was a whole flock of nieces and nephews; but they lived somewhere else, some of them even in Australia, which is about as far away as you can get. Barbara along with her sister Karen were the ones that mattered most to Aunt Harriet. They were the only nieces who lived in the

Bay Area. Their own mother, Harriet's sister Ruth, had died of breast cancer some twenty years earlier, and ever since then these two women had been close to their aunt. She was, I guess, a kind of substitute mother for them. She and Barbara were very fond of each other.

Karen's last name was Bridges. She was 50-something, and she was a widow. I know nothing about the late Mr. Bridges. I think he died quite young. The marriage had produced a daughter, whose name escapes me. Anyway, this daughter was married, to a dentist, and was living in Cleveland, Ohio, with her husband and I think some children. She has absolutely no part to play in this story, so you can forget about her, if you wish.

Aunt Harriet had died early in August. The conversation with Barbara, the one I'm telling you about, took place more or less on Friday toward the end of August, give or take a day or two. I don't remember the exact date. I could look it up, but the precise day doesn't matter.

My first impression, to be sure, was that the whole idea, about somebody murdering Aunt Harriet, was completely absurd. But Barbara seemed quite serious. I felt I had to go along with her so I asked, "What exactly did she say, Barbara? When you had that conversation, you know, the one where you felt she was, uh, in danger. You haven't told me the facts."

"I'll give you the whole story, Frank. But first, I want to back up a bit, and fill you in on some aspects of our situation. My aunt—well, I don't want to say she had changed in recent months; but in a way, she was different; she seemed worried, preoccupied. Oh, she tried to hide it, but I could tell... she had something on her mind."

"And she didn't tell you what it was."

"No, she didn't. Maybe it would be more accurate to say she *wouldn't*. I spoke to her about it, several times. I said, Harriet, what's on your mind? You seem so... troubled."

"And what did she say?"

"Nothing. She changed the subject. But once, we were having dinner together, oh, maybe a month or so before she died, she did open up a little bit. She said something, well, it sounded very strange to me. She said: Barbara, I've done some terrible things in my life. I said, I can't believe that, Aunt Harriet. You're a wonderful, wise, loving person. She said, maybe I am now, thank you for saying that, but I wasn't always. I made... mistakes. I said, do you want to tell me about them? What I meant, Frank—I didn't want to pry; but I thought, she's bothered by something, and maybe it would help, you know, if she talked about it. But she said, no, she'd rather not."

"You got nothing more out of her?"

"Only this: she repeated that she had done some terrible things, and she said, I'm paying for it now. She said it again: I'm paying for what I did, Barbara; and in some ways, I'm willing to make up my wrongs. But the price is going up, and I don't know if I can do it anymore."

"What did you say?"

"I told her I loved her, and I wanted to help her, and if she was in any kind of trouble, she could call on me, and please do that, and I said, this is very mysterious, I have no idea what you're talking about, and I said, you know, Aunt Harriet, you can tell me *anything*, you can trust me, I repeated that; but she just smiled and said, well, maybe when the time comes; and that was that."

"And you have no idea what she was referring to?" "None at all," Barbara said. "And then: well, then came this other business. It was, I think, a Saturday night. I'm sure it was. I took her to the movies. I don't remember what we saw. Some comedy. Aunt Harriet didn't mind sex in the movies, but she didn't like violence. I picked her up, we had a quick bite in a Chinese restaurant, then we went to the movies. Aunt Harriet seemed very quiet—not at all like her usual self. She was quite a character; well, you remember; you knew her, Frank. We had coffee after the movie, in Palo Alto, on University Avenue. One of those cafes. Usually she wanted to go right home, go to bed. She wasn't a night person. But she said, let's get some coffee, Barbara, I want to talk to you. Her mood was... funny, you know; distant, sort of. It was like that other time. I said,

Harriet, now I'm sure of it, there's something on your mind. She said, yes there is. So we went for the coffee.

"And so there we were, sitting and drinking our coffee, and I waited for her to talk. But then she seemed to change her mind, said she didn't want to talk about it after all. I was getting worried. I said, is it your health, Aunt Harriet? She said: well, no. Not exactly. I asked her, is it connected with that other thing, the thing you mentioned, you know, when you told me you made some mistakes. She said, well, yes, it is. Then she said something terrifically odd."

"What was that?" "She said: 'if something happens to me...' then she broke off the sentence. I said, what do you mean, what's going to happen to you, you're not telling me something—have you been to the doctor, I know that something's wrong. I remembered, I had gone with her, to the doctor—I mean, I dropped her off there, the week before, and picked her up, at the clinic, you know? The Palo Alto Clinic. That's where she went, for checkups and things. I thought, maybe she got bad news. From lab tests, maybe. But she said, oh, no, it's nothing like that, but.... Then she wouldn't say any more for a while. Just stirred her coffee with a spoon. It was very strange. I told her she *had* to confide in me, she just had to. Finally she said, I don't know if I ought to tell you. You see, I'm... pretty frightened. Or words to that effect. Of course I was startled, I asked her, frightened? Yes, she said, I'm really afraid. Afraid of what? Of somebody? Is somebody trying to hurt you?"

"Why did you ask her that? What made you think somebody wanted to hurt her?"

"Well, Frank, I had a reason. Because of something that happened a while before that...."

"Something that happened? What?"

"Actually, more than one thing. The first was... well, let's skip that part for now. I'll tell you some other time. Maybe. The other thing was this. About a week before she died, and just before this conversation, I was driving by, and decided to drop in and see her. I used to do that a lot. Well, to my surprise, there was a police car parked out in front. I got quite scared. What were the police doing there?

"Naturally, I was alarmed. I thought, my God, something's happened, something's wrong. So I rushed inside, and there was Aunt Harriet, talking to some policemen, two of them I think. They were all sitting in the living room. She looked extremely nervous. I said, 'Aunt Harriet, what's the problem?' She said, 'never mind.' She said to the policemen, this is my niece. They seemed to be just about through, with whatever it was they were doing. They got up and left the house. I said, 'Aunt Harriet, you've got to tell me what this is all about. Why were those policemen here?' But she absolutely wouldn't say."

"And... you still don't know?"

"Not a clue. Still: you can imagine my reaction... when she made this other comment. I tried to get her to say more, but she said I would have to wait. She said, yes, she was afraid of somebody, somebody wanted to harm her, those were her very words. She said maybe she would tell me later. I was very alarmed. I said, if you mean what you're saying, Harriet, then we should do something."

"And what did she say?"

"She said, no, not now; maybe later."

"And you don't know what she was referring to?"

"I had a vague idea. I don't want to share it with you, though—at least not yet, Frank... not until I know more, OK? Anyway: I said, we have to go to the police. But she laughed. She said, that wouldn't do any good. I was sorry I mentioned the police, because it flashed into my mind, the police were *already* involved, somehow.... I probed a bit; but Aunt Harriet was a stubborn woman, and she changed the subject. A week later she was dead."

"It could be a coincidence, Barbara. Her dying, I mean. She could have had a heart attack. Old people do, after all."

"Yes... but still, she was very healthy. I know she was old, but... I talked to her doctor yesterday. I asked him point blank what he thought about Aunt Harriet dying, her health, and so on. He admitted he was surprised when he got the news. You see, he was away at the time. He was on vacation, and he found out she was dead when he came back. That was his word: surprised. I asked him why. She seemed in such good shape, he said, for her age. But then he said, well, after all, she *was* 83 or 84, he didn't remember her exact age; and sometimes these things come on all of a sudden."

"That's very true," I said, "take my grandmother—"

But Barbara was not about to take my grandmother. She plunged ahead: "So, all in all, it was very suspicious, don't you think? And this business with the will.... You have to admit, Frank, there's something fishy going on."

Yes, I had to admit it. Aunt Harriet, as I said, had been a client of mine. I drew up her Last Will and Testament. Or what I thought was her Last Will and Testament.

It was an easy and straightforward will. Aunt Harriet was quite a rich woman. A very rich woman, in fact. She inherited money from her husband, Joseph Wingate, who died about twenty years before her. Joseph Wingate had been a businessman, and a very successful one; and when he died, he left everything to his widow. Harriet was shrewd and careful; she made sure that the money kept growing. She lived modestly, for a woman of her wealth—not that she scrimped and saved, but she lived within her very ample means.

Joseph, for example, had left her some real estate in Silicon Valley and the very large house the two of them shared. She sold the house at an enormous profit and bought a smaller house, where she lived until she died. She kept the rest of the real estate, and sold it off gradually, always for enormous profits.

Well, part of this was luck. Everybody wants to live in Silicon Valley or anywhere around the San Francisco area. Can you blame them? No ice and snow; and in summer, no mosquitoes and no humidity. No wonder people flock to northern California. I'm so lucky I bought my house a long time ago. Today, you just can't touch a house in the Bay Area; they're astronomically expensive. The most modest sort of bungalow is a fortune. We have too many millionaires and billionaires around. I mean, money that would buy a mansion in Buffalo or Fargo wouldn't get you a mobile home in a trailer park out here. And while the real estate market was booming, even an idiot could make money out of real estate. And Harriet Wingate was no idiot. She knew when to buy and when to sell.

In addition, she had a nice portfolio of stocks and bonds; and she paid close attention to the market. Her investments had grown to many millions of dollars. I think twenty million, at least. We won't know for sure until we prepare an inventory.

The will. Yes. Nothing startling. She left money to a few charities, and small gifts to some of her friends; also a few thousand dollars to each of her far-off nieces and nephews. The rest of it, the bulk of the estate, went one-half to her husband Tommy, and one quarter each to her two favorite nieces, Barbara and Karen.

She named Barbara executor. If Barbara died or resigned, Karen would take over. Apparently Tommy, whatever his talents, was not her idea of someone she wanted to manage her estate.

Quite a straightforward will, in other words. Nothing fancy. The only oddity *was* the money she left to her husband, Tommy. Of course, there's nothing unusual about leaving half your money to your spouse. It's quite normal. What wasn't normal was this particular spouse. I don't mean to imply anything was wrong with Tommy—for now, I'll just mention that Tommy was 23 years old. Not a day older. Harriet Wingate, you will remember, was in her 80's. At least sixty years difference. That's a lot, if you ask me. In other words, they were not your ordinary married couple. They were June and December. He was June.

June and December does happen; but usually, it's the other way around. Rich old goats marry trophy wives. Rich old ladies, for the most part, have more sense.

Right now, there was an even greater problem with the will: nobody could find it. It had vanished into thin air. Barbara looked; Karen looked; other people looked. Not a trace of it.

I was the one who prepared the will. Harriet Wingate was my client—had been for years. Not that I ever did much for her. I forget who recommended me to her. Mostly, I wrote her wills. This was a new will, but it wasn't much different from the one before it. She changed some of the smaller gifts, and she added a bit for the nieces and nephews, even the ones in Australia. She also added a friend or two, and dropped a few, including an old friend named Hilda. Harriet told me, it was because of Hilda's daughter's wedding. Hilda told her they were inviting 500 people. And it was a second marriage! "I said to Hilda, this is disgusting, you're spending a fortune. And the actual wedding, it was so vulgar, they had this loud music, some rock and roll band, the noise could wake the dead. And the bride was so drunk she could hardly stand up. I told Hilda I found the whole thing repulsive, and she laughed and said, it's the way things are these days. Well, I thought, if she's throwing her money around like that, she doesn't need mine." And that was the end of Hilda's modest legacy.

She also dropped a charity here, added a charity there. "That fund for people with diabetes," she said to me, "I used to like them, Joseph had diabetes, did you know that? But they keep sending me things, calendars, shopping bags, it's like Hilda, they're just wasting money on that junk; I'm not leaving them a cent." She switched to Parkinson's disease and kidney dialysis.

Harriet had strong ideas about everything. She left a few thousand dollars to Edna her cleaning lady, and to a delivery boy who brought her groceries; she didn't even know his name, I had to call Safeway to find out. He works hard, she said, and he always calls me ma'am. He'll amount to something some day.

I took the instructions, wrote the will (it wasn't much work), and Harriet came to my office to sign it. She seemed perfectly normal to me. She was dressed in a plain black dress, with a bright yellow belt. She wore a strand of pearls. Celia, my wife, could tell you more about what she was wearing. I'm tone deaf when it comes to women's fashions, if you know what I mean.

Harriet seated herself, we exchanged some small talk, and then we got down to business. I showed her the will, I explained what was in it, I read her the relevant parts, I skipped over the dull technical things, and made it all as clear as I could. She nodded her head. I asked her if this was what she wanted. She said yes. She was ready and willing to sign.

I needed two witnesses. My practice was to call in two young lawyers, young women, associates at a firm in the next building. I'm a solo practitioner, I don't have partners. The head of the firm next door was an old friend of mine, Richie Stern. He does shopping centers and condominiums. We don't compete, and he's happy to lend his associates, when we need witnesses for wills.

The whole thing went smoothly—why not? It always goes smoothly. There's no magic to it; it's completely routine. Harriet signed; the two young lawyers added their names as witnesses; , and that was that.

When we were finished, I thanked the witnesses, Sonia and Andrea, offered them coffee, which they refused, and we said goodbye. I smiled at Harriet Wingate. I always worry about elderly clients who come in to sign their wills. I don't want them to think about dying. It's too morbid.

"You'll live twenty more years," I said to her. "We'll have dozens more wills, Harriet. I promise you."

She said: "You're a liar, Frank. Dozens more? I'm 83. But... well, you're a good man. And I'm glad we've got this over and done with."

"And the old will? Be sure to destroy it, won't you?"

She nodded. Then I told Aunt Harriet it would be best if I kept the original will; put it in my vault. That's where I keep my clients' wills, if they let me. I never liked the fact that she had always kept her wills in her home. Houses aren't safe places for wills. "Really, Harriet," I said. "Leave it with me, the will. I do this all the time. It's... pretty standard."

But Aunt Harriet refused. She said, she wanted it where she could look at it; she'd put it in a drawer, and not to worry.

"You can look at a xerox," I said. "You can read it three times a day, if you like. At least put the original in a safe deposit box; keeping it at home, Harriet, I don't advise that. It's too risky."

But Harriet was a stubborn woman. "No, Frank, she said, I appreciate your concern. But I'll keep the original with me, thank you."

"OK, Harriet," I said. "But, for instance: suppose there's a fire?"

"I don't believe in fires," she said. There'll be no fire."

That was Aunt Harriet. I dropped the subject. I never argue with a client. Especially a client as rich as Harriet Wingate. She took the will with her, in a manila envelope. And it disappeared into a kind of black hole.

2

Aunt Harriet, as I said, lived in a small house—sort of an overgrown cottage—in the city of Palo Alto. It was a two-story house. She lived alone. She could have had a bigger house and a housekeeper, but she wanted privacy and a kind of independence. Her tastes did not run to the grandiose. Edna, the cleaning lady, came every day (I think); but there was no live-in help. It was a pretty house, neat, well-ordered. I remember the beautiful curtains and drapes—all bright canary yellow; and the yellow wallpaper. It gave the place a cheerful look, all shiny and bright; forward-looking, and even a bit bold. On the other hand, I think some of the furniture was fairly antiquated. Family heirlooms; and perhaps quite valuable. Aunt Harriet came from a very old family.

"She was a Spively," Karen said to me once. Karen was Barbara's sister. I think I mentioned that.

"Right. A Spively." I didn't know what a Spively was. It could have been anything. It turned out to be the name of a family, the sort of family that knows who its ancestors are.

"Wingate was her married name, of course," Karen said. "She was born a Spively." She could see I was unimpressed. I tried to look as if it meant something to me, but I failed, as I usually do at that sort of thing. Karen went on to tell me, in great detail: "The Spively's came over on the Mayflower. Literally. Peleg Spively was his name, the ancestor. He married Hepzibah Witherspoon. My mother and Aunt Harriet were direct descendants of Peleg and Hepzibah Spively."

For myself, I was the descendant, as far as I know, of a long line of peddlers and nobodies. My ancestors most definitely did *not* come over on the Mayflower. They came on some sort of cattle-boat, I suppose, in the late nineteenth century, one of those boats full of lice and dirt, with zillions of people crammed into the hold of the ship. I suppose they were part of the huddled masses yearning to be free. In any event, I never had much interest in family background. My grandparents died when I was young. That could be one reason. Some people have grandparents who talk a lot about the old days; and maybe that's why they become hooked on genealogy.

Karen, unlike me, was obsessed with the subject. It was one of her chief occupations. "I'm writing a history of the Spively family," she said. "I'm enormously proud of them. It's people like Peleg and Hepzibah who made this country great."

"Did you hear a lot about the Spively's from Aunt Harriet?" I asked.

Karen laughed. "Good grief, no. She couldn't care less. Aunt Harriet had no sense of family history. She despised all that, to tell you the truth. Quite the opposite. She once said to me, Karen, if you dig long enough, you'll find skeletons in the closet. She said, she'd rather not dwell on the past. No, Frank, I'm the only one in the family that really cares. And I do care, deeply. I think family is... almost everything. It's tradition, it's... well, it's in the blood, don't you think?"

I nodded my head in agreement. I always agree with my clients, unless they say something about the law, in which case I set them straight, but gently. I wondered if Karen honestly thought that being a Spively made you better than all those other people, the millions and millions of non-Spivelys. I hope not.

But I see I'm digressing. At least you probably *think* I'm digressing. You probably think it doesn't matter to this story that Harriet Wingate was born a Spively. Actually, it does, but that comes a lot later on.

Anyway, I was telling you something about Harriet Wingate's house. I won't bore you with details. The basic facts are these: it was a two-story house, rather conventional. Downstairs was a guest-room, a living room, a kitchen and a half-bath. Upstairs was the main bedroom, which Harriet occupied, also a bathroom, and two small rooms, one of which Harriet used as a kind of study. Not that she studied anything. But she wrote letters at a desk, and the desk had a locked drawer, in which she kept important papers like her will. Except that the will wasn't there.

I want to mention again the fact that she lived alone. Her husband, Tommy, lived somewhere else. At one time, he did live in the house—in the guest room downstairs. But about a year before Harriet died he moved out. More about this later.

Anyway, Harriet Wingate was all alone when she died. She died in her sleep. Or was murdered, if you believe Barbara's version, in which case she wasn't alone when she died. In the morning, the cleaning lady, Edna, came to the house as usual. She was a heavyset lady—I'd seen her once or twice; a nice woman who had been cleaning for Harriet for years and years. Like so many women who cleaned houses, she had had a miserable life, which she never hesitated to tell you about. Her husband, who drank himself to death. Her oldest son who got in with the wrong crowd, and was sitting in jail. Her daughter's many pregnancies. She lived across the bay and had to travel a long distance to get to Harriet's house. But she liked Harriet; Harriet was good to her.

Anyway, that morning, she let herself in with her key, as usual, and went about her work. But when she got upstairs—well, you can imagine the scene. Harriet Wingate was still lying in bed, completely dead.

It upset Edna and she started screaming and crying, but nobody heard her of course. (Barbara told me this part of the story). Then she calmed down, called a doctor—as if a doctor could do anything with a dead woman and of course phoned Barbara. Barbara, as it happened, wasn't home; she was with her exercise group at a gym. Then Edna called Karen, told her what had happened; and Karen came right over. Not that there was anything *she* could do. I guess they eventually did contact Barbara—she was home an hour later—and the two of them started calling the other relatives. They also called Tommy, who was, after all, Harriet's husband, and began arranging for the funeral and so on.

Tommy, by the way, played no part in any of the arrangements, the funeral, the family affairs and so on. The two sisters simply took over. I note that for the record.

I was one of the people they called, and naturally I said how sorry I was and what a wonderful woman Harriet Wingate had been, and all that; and I expressed my sorrow and my empathy. I don't want to sound cynical: I really was sorry Harriet had passed on, and Barbara and Karen felt genuine grief, I'm sure of that, they were very close, after all; and I suppose for them it was therapeutic to get down to details, the funeral, the estate, and the rest of that.

Anyway, Barbara and I went to the house the very next day—the body had gone to the funeral parlor—I'm not big on dead bodies; and Barbara and I had breakfast together and talked about the estate, at least in a general way. The will, at least the will I drafted, named Barbara as executor. Barbara let us in with her key—I stress this fact, because it became relevant, later on, to talk about who had a key and who did not.

I was struck by how neat the house was. And how quiet. Of course it was quiet, but it seemed unnaturally quiet. I know I'm talking nonsense. If I didn't know that Harriet was dead, it wouldn't have seemed any different from any other house. But it gave me a creepy feeling. It seemed so... still, so frozen in time, like a museum. Maybe I'm just being sentimental.

Anyway, that's when we went to look for the will. The Last Will and Testament of Harriet Wingate. The one I drew up, all legal and proper. We looked, all over the house. The will was simply not there. We looked in all the usual places: nothing. First of all, we had gone into the study, and looked in the drawers of the desk. The drawers were locked, but Barbara had a key. We searched every drawer. We found some papers and letters, and a deed to the house, but not much of any real interest.

Only one thing: something rather surprising. It had nothing to do with the will. It seems that Harriet Wingate kept, locked in one of the drawers of her desk, a manila folder, with newspaper clippings. We were busy searching for a will, but I couldn't help looking at the clippings, all yellowing with age. There was, for instance, her late husband's obituary. And a story, from the local newspaper, about him, two columns long. And a picture of Joseph Wingate, looking very old. There were other clippings about the family; an item by Karen in a local newspaper, about the Spively family, and how Karen was tracing their ancestry, and so on, all about the fact that there was a southern branch and a New England branch of the Spively's; I barely glanced at this.

But then there was something quite different: old clippings, seven or eight years old, from an Arizona newspaper. One clipping told about a horrendous crime near Phoenix. Two men, a woman, and an adolescent boy had been on a crime spree, robbing stores in and around Phoenix. They were caught but escaped. On the run, they hijacked a car, and kidnapped a young couple with two kids, who had been driving the car. The gang drove out to the desert, and murdered the family or tried to. One of the kids survived to tell the tale. Another clipping told a follow-up story: how the police caught up with the gang, and there was a gun battle, and one of the gang was killed. I couldn't help wondering: how was this connected to Harriet Wingate? Why had she preserved these particular clippings, for so long, in a locked drawer in her desk?

"Did you find anything?" Barbara asked.

I was embarrassed, put down the folder and continued the search. I found nothing; at any rate, no will.

I asked Barbara if anybody else had a key to this dresser and to the drawers. She thought not, but wasn't sure. Anybody besides Harriet Wingate, I mean. Her own key was in a black leather purse, along with her house keys and a lot of the other stuff women carry in their purses. And the purse was right where we expected it to be—in her bedroom.

Not that I thought about foul play or anything of the sort, not at the time. I just wondered why the will wasn't there.

"You don't think somebody stole it?" Barbara asked. "The drawer was locked."

"Right. But that kind of flimsy lock isn't much of an obstacle, not to a professional," I said. Of course I didn't know what I was talking about. For me, the lock would have been an insuperable obstacle.

"Where *could* that will be?" Barbara asked.

Well, one obvious answer would be: in Harriet's safe deposit box. Or boxes: she had two of them, in two different banks in Palo Alto, one on California Avenue, another on El Camino Real. The vault keys were in a little envelope, in that desk drawer. We had no trouble getting entry, because the boxes were in the joint names of Harriet Wingate and Barbara Homans.

"I didn't have the key, actually," Barbara said. "But Aunt Harriet wanted my name on these boxes, in case something happened to her. And... something did," she said, and reached for her handkerchief. She began sobbing quietly.

I find grief very embarrassing. I don't know how to deal with it. It's a male deficiency—I know that. My wife Celia is much better at situations of this kind; she knows how to behave. Anyway, we checked out both boxes. In each bank, we took the box into the little cubicles they give you, and we examined everything inside the box. We made lists and catalogued everything. There were stocks and bonds. Some of the stock certificates were quite old and beautiful. Wonderful engravings. Nowadays, a person's portfolio has been reduced to electronic blips. The poetry is gone. Harriet had arranged everything neatly. There were also all sorts of legal documents: a copy of Joseph Wingate's death certificate, in an envelope, along with a yellowed clipping from the newspaper—another version of his obituary. There were also deeds to various pieces of real estate—all of them sold by now. But in neither bank, in neither safe deposit box, was there the slightest sign of anything like a will.

Of course, Aunt Harriet might have torn the will up. There's always that possibility. She had taken it home, against my advice; and she could have destroyed it. You can do that, you know. Nothing to it, and it's perfectly legal. You just tear the will to pieces, or you burn it, you throw it out in the trash, or you flush it down the toilet. That's the end of the will, legally speaking. You've revoked it, as we lawyers say.

She could have done one of those things. In that case, the will would be gone without a trace. But somehow I doubted this. Aunt Harriet was very careful about financial and legal affairs. I'm sure she would have told me about it—she would have called me on the phone, at the very least, and told me what she had done.

This is the way I felt at the time—the way I felt when Barbara and I left Bank No. 2, and the realization sank in that there was no will to be found *anywhere*; that, as far as we knew, she died without a will. As you'll see, I was wrong about many, many things—things having to do with Harriet Wingate, and about other people too.... But at the time, I was simply puzzled and confused.

Suppose she hadn't torn up her will; in that case, what could have happened to the blasted thing? You don't just go around losing wills. They're too precious. Too important. But whatever happened, the brute fact remained: we had no will in front of us.

We had been discussing this very situation, in my office, just before Barbara brought up her strange idea: the idea that somebody killed Aunt Harriet. Aunt Harriet had been dead a few weeks, as I told you. Of course, the will issue had surfaced very quickly. We had to open an estate for Harriet—a will might turn up later. I had my doubts; but this was an estate of millions of dollars, and we had to do *something*. So I did open an estate, and I persuaded the court to appoint Barbara as the administrator, at least on a temporary basis.

She was, after all, a close relative. Tommy, the surviving spouse, under the law, had the right to serve as administrator; but apparently he didn't want to, and he was perfectly happy to let Barbara have the job. That's what Barbara told me, and she had Tommy write me a note, saying he declined to serve. The note was scrawled, in big letters, the way a fifth grader would write. Half the words were misspelled. Tommy, I gathered, was no genius.

Anyway, that was the situation we were facing. The estate had to be opened, and there was a lot of business to be taken care of, will or no will. I explained to Barbara what her duties were, what to do about dividends, how she could pay bills, and out of what account. How to handle the whole estate, in other words. She listened and took notes. When I was more or less done with my spiel, that's when Barbara dropped her bombshell.

"Wait a minute," I said, "do you think the missing will is... well, connected to this, uh, *theory* of yours?"

"This *theory*?"

"This idea. This suspicion. What you just told me," I said.

"I absolutely do. Somebody tore up that will or stole it. And it wasn't Aunt Harriet," she said.

"But who would do a thing like that?" I asked.

"Ah, that's the question," she said. "But *somebody* did. I just *know* she kept the will in that dresser drawer. It just had to be there. And you said yourself, it wouldn't be much of a trick to break into that drawer. Who knows? Anybody who came in the house might have gotten hold of that will."

"But who was that? Who came into the house?"

"Well: Tommy for one," she said.

"Tommy? Her husband?"

"Naturally. He had a key."

But this didn't seem very likely to me. Why would Tommy steal her will and tear it up? The will left him half the estate. He and Aunt Harriet had not been married very long and California is a community property state. He was entitled to half the community property; but I didn't think that would amount to much. Basically, tearing up the will would probably make him much worse off.

"He doesn't have a motive," I said. "That will left him millions of dollars."

"Did he know that?"

"Well, if he stole the will, he could read it, couldn't he? And he'd see it there, in black and white."

"It didn't say, I leave millions of dollars to Tommy."

"It gave him, roughly, half the estate. He could figure out that was real money. He must have known Harriet was rich."

"Well, he could have had a reason."

"Maybe," I said. "Who else had access to the house?"

"Frank, I don't know. I did. Edna did. There could have been other people. Karen, for one."

"Did Karen have a key?"

"Karen wouldn't do a thing like that."

"I didn't say she would."

"Anyway," Barbara said. "I'm not sure she had a key. But it could have been some other visitor. How would I know who came and went at Aunt Harriet's?"

How indeed. The question was: who gained if the will was destroyed? Not Barbara and Karen: like Tommy, they lost a lot of money in the process. So did the friends who would have gotten something under the will. If no will showed up, then Harriet Wingate died intestate, as the legal term goes. Tommy would get a share. I'd have to look up exactly how much, and the rest I suppose would go to all the nieces and nephews, because they were the closest living kin. I'm not sure how many there were. Harriet Wingate had had a sister, Barbara's mother, now dead. There were two brothers, older brothers, and both of *them* were dead. The nieces and nephews were scattered all over—Sydney Australia, Cincinnati, other exotic places. Karen and Barbara were the only ones who lived in the Bay Area. I think I told you that.

I made a mental note to check the California Probate Code and confirm this, I mean that the nieces and nephews would get the estate. I work with the Code all the time; I do a lot of estates work, maybe more of that line of work than anything else, but I certainly don't know the Code by heart. It's a thousand pages long. Most of it, of course, is incredibly dull. Maybe all of it. Nobody reads the Probate Code for pleasure.

"You're awfully quiet," Barbara said. "What are you thinking about?"

"The will... or rather that there isn't any will," I said.

"I know. It's a mystery, isn't it?" she said.

"It's not *like* Harriet. To be so careless with a thing like that. Not like her at all."

"You're right. I mean, it's really all wrong. Aunt Harriet would never, never let that happen. Not to have a will. She wanted us—me and Karen—to have the money. I'm sure of that. I'm totally convinced somebody got in and tore up the will."

She was right about Harriet's wishes. When we discussed her will, she made it crystal clear: she wanted Barbara and her sister Karen to have half the estate. She also definitely wanted to leave money to Tommy. That was equally clear; but I didn't stress this point. Barbara had said nothing about Tommy.

"Barbara," I said, "I know what you're saying. But... it's a serious thing, to tear up somebody's will."

"Very serious, I'm sure. So is stealing and murder and so on, but they happen."

"That's true," I said. "Not that I've ever come across such a thing, I mean, where somebody deliberately tore up somebody else's will. Not in all my years as a lawyer."

"There's a first time for everything," she said.

"It's weird, I admit it," I said. "Still, Aunt Harriet did some weird things, didn't she?"

"Weird things? What sorts of things?"

I was going to mention marrying somebody 60 years her junior, but I held my tongue. This might be a sore subject. "Never mind.... Anyway, there's nothing we can do about the will. And, frankly, we can't do anything about your idea that somebody murdered your aunt."

"You're telling me to forget it? Not to do anything about it?"

"I guess I am. Unless something else comes up, something more specific."

"Honestly, Frank!" she said; her voice dripped disappointment. But what else could I do or say? Murder was hardly my specialty. And this wasn't even murder... at least, I didn't think so. Just an old lady, dying in her sleep. We changed the subject, talked more about the estate, the assets, what Barbara's role was going to be, and so on.

She left around five o'clock. I had to see another client, who had been waiting impatiently for me in the outer office. I spent about half an hour with the client. I did a little bit of paperwork, then I hurried home for dinner.

Celia had invited some guests to join us. Celia teaches in the local high school. The assistant principal, whose name was Jerry something—I forget his last name—came with his wife, Marilyn, who was very fat. Fat, and extremely quiet. Jerry Something always did all of the talking. Celia made a fish stew. It was one of her specialties. Some people don't like fish; but she felt that was their problem, not hers.

I rushed home, because it would be unfair to Celia if I came too late to help out; even worse if I arrived after the guests did. When I got home, Celia was frantically working. She was behind schedule and I had to pitch in immediately, cutting carrots and cucumbers and tossing the salad. The evening was boring, but distracting. Celia and Jerry Something talked, or rather gossiped, about what went on at the school. Marilyn and I were basically furniture. But for the time being at least, I forgot all about Barbara, Aunt Harriet, and the missing will.

The next day, however, I got a strange phone call from a lawyer named Peter Elver, and the case of Harriet Wingate took the first of many surprising turns.

About the author

Lawrence Friedman is a professor of law at Stanford University. He teaches courses in American legal history and law and society. He is the author of *A History of American Law*, *Crime and Punishment in American History*, *The Human Rights Culture*, and *Total Justice*, among other works. He recently published *Dead Hands: A Social History of Wills, Trusts, and Inheritances*, a subject which is the backbone of Frank May's (fictional) practice.

Visit us at *www.qpbooks.com.*